Uncoverings

2016

Volume 37 of the Research Papers
of the American Quilt Study Group

Edited by Lynne Zacek Bassett

Presented at Tempe, Arizona
September 14-18, 2016

Published by the American Quilt Study Group
1610 L. Street
Lincoln, NE 68508

Manufactured in the United States

Uncoverings is indexed in:
America: History and Life
ARTbibliographies
BHA (Bibliography of the History of Art)
Clothing and Textile Arts Index
Feminist Periodicals
Historical Abstracts
MLA International Bibliography
Sociological Abstracts

ISBN 10 digit 1-877859-32-x
ISBN 13 digit 978-1-877859-32-8
ISSN 0277-0628
Library of Congress catalog number: 81-649486

Cover image: Pearl Harris Evans, Lattice Quilt, Macon, North
Carolina, c. 1951–1958. Satin acetate florist ribbon, pieced. 63 x
86 inches. Made in memory of Willie Raymond Riggan,
North Carolina Quilt Project, courtesy of the North Carolina
Museum of History.

Table of Contents

Foreword

A FACEBOOK FRIEND AND I have recently been debating the term "artisan quilter," as used by Pottery Barn to promote its new line of designer quilts. Is every quilter an artisan? If every quilter is an artisan, does that mean every quilt has artistic merit? No matter which side of the debate you take, it must be acknowledged that the quilters presented in this volume of *Uncoverings* put careful thought and artistry into their quilts. Their stitches give voice to personal messages of mourning, spirituality, fear, pride, delight, anger, and determination.

Peggy Hazard provides the AQSG 2016 Seminar attendees in Tempe, Arizona, with an intimate look at the difficult and divisive issue of illegal immigration in the state. Using the discarded clothing of migrants making the dangerous desert crossing from Mexico into Arizona, The Migrant Quilt Project commemorates the lives lost under the unforgiving sun and opens a conversation not only about humanity, grief, and generosity, but about public policy. Unlike the faceless and sometimes even nameless people commemorated by The Migrant Quilt Project, the makers of the funeral ribbon quilts studied by Diana Bell-Kite memorialized their own family members. Bell-Kite documents the southern practice of collecting the ribbons from funeral floral arrangements in order to stitch together a treasured keepsake of the ceremony as well as the loved one. The demise of the practice with the floral industry's shift to thinner, less-stable ribbon material has made this a bygone tradition—important to document now, before these inherently fragile quilts disintegrate or are forgotten by families separated by time or distance from the maker.

Mourning is not always due to the death of a beloved friend or family member. The loss of a dream can also cause profound sadness. Jonathan Gregory examines this sort of mourning in his essay, "Why Ernest Haight Made Quilts." In the face of the 1930s economic depression that took away his career hopes and caused severe stress over his family's well-being, Ernest Haight turned his engineering skills to quilt design in order not to "crack up." His success as a quiltmaker not only satisfied his own intellectual goals, but also his desire to be useful to his community. In contrast to Haight's difficult situation, in that same decade of the Great Depression, wealthy socialite Mildred Potter Lissauer also set out to prove her talents as a quilt designer. Sandy Staebell offers an in-depth study of Lissauer's colonial revival *Godey Quilt,* discussing its inspiration, sources, and production. Staebell presents new information about this well-known quilt—how Lissauer developed her design, and how other talented needlewomen fulfilled Lissauer's vision. Both Ernest Haight and Mildred Potter Lissauer sought praise and validation of their work—Haight, through his county and state agricultural fairs, and Lissauer through national competitions and publications.

The decades following the Great Depression were generally quiet ones in American quilt history, but there was a significant ramping-up of interest as the country got closer to the Bicentennial of 1976. Colleen Hall-Patton examines how quilts were perceived by the writers for American women's magazines between 1940 and 1971, focusing particularly on the beginnings of feminist values associated with the practice of quilting—quilting not just within the context of homemaking, but quiltmaking as a legitimate and worthy outlet for a woman's creativity (or "artisanry," to return to the opening debate of this Foreword), personal expression, and time. Hall-Patton ends her study just prior to the beginning of the Quilt Revival in the 1970s, as large numbers of women rediscovered this textile art as a medium for more than just home decoration or warmth. The quilts of Mary Catherine Lamb are a dynamic result of the growth of the Quilt Revival. Susan Stanley assigns Lamb's work—which is only now gaining a widespread appreciation for its imagination, beauty, and imagery—to its deserved place within the Studio Art Quilt movement of the 1990s and 2000s. Lamb created tributes to her Catholic upbringing that were both honorific and humorous. Constructed of unusual fabrics gathered from thrift shops and yard sales, she sliced, skewed, and arranged the pieces to create slightly off-kilter images of biblical saints and monsters.

I would argue that an important element of art is emotion—the emotion with which it is imbued by its creator, and the emotion it evokes in the viewer. While (in my humble opinion) not all quilts rise to the level of art or even artisanry, this volume of *Uncoverings* offers significant fodder for consideration of the importance of quilts as art and emotional expression.

—Lynne Zacek Bassett

What the Eye Doesn't See, Doesn't Move the Heart: Migrant Quilts of Southern Arizona

Peggy J. Hazard

Illegal immigration has become a humanitarian crisis on both sides of the Atlantic. One fact often left out of the conversation about migration to the United States from Mexico is that thousands of undocumented—and frequently unidentified—men, women and children have died in the Southern Arizona deserts since the imposition of trade and border policies in the 1990s. The Migrant Quilt Project is a grassroots effort in Tucson, Arizona, to collect clothing discarded in the desert by migrants and reuse it to create quilts recording the names of these unacknowledged victims of the border crisis. The quilts are intended to memorialize the dead, reveal the severity of the tragedy, and inspire people to support compassionate policy change. Based on interviews with the project's founder, the quilts' creators, immigration activists, and the author's personal experience making a Migrant Quilt, this paper tells the story of the project's origins and the effects of the quilts on those who have made and viewed them. The quilts are invaluable documents of a particular time and place in history and this paper discusses them within the contexts of art made from migrant clothing, border-themed textile art, and the heritage of socially-conscious quiltmaking.

Death in the Desert

The Huachuca Mountains are one of southern Arizona's "sky island" ranges, where high forested peaks are surrounded by a sea of desert. Extending northwest from the United States/Mexico border, the mountains are a popular recreation area, especially for birdwatchers who flock to Ramsey Canyon, and for hikers, who can set off there at the southern entrance to the Arizona Trail. But in 2005, when longtime Tucsonan Jody Ipsen and a friend camped in the Huachucas, they came across something

Fig. 1. *Pile of Migrant Artifacts—Arivaca, Arizona*, c. 2005. Photograph by Michael Hyatt.

they did not expect to see in the scenic wilderness: discarded baby diapers, bottles, backpacks and clothes strewn along a trail. Ipsen was horrified to learn that the trash had been left behind by border crossers and that the trails in the Huachucas are a main travel route for undocumented immigrants from Mexico.

Ipsen's experience in the mountains sparked her curiosity and she began to educate herself about illegal migration from Mexico. She researched the 1990s trade policies that motivated dramatic increases in northward immigration and discovered that subsequent border crackdowns funneled migrants into a dangerous open section of the border in Southern Arizona where many of them died from exposure and dehydration. Ipsen felt compassion for the deceased migrants and their families, particularly for those whose remains were not identifiable. Although a majority of migrants are young men, she particularly wanted to understand why women left their homes, risking everything to go to the United States. She even traveled to Central America and Mexico to meet people affected by the immigration crisis, focusing on the families of women who died.

Ipsen volunteered with local humanitarian organizations, walking migrant trails with the Tucson Samaritans and No More Deaths, encountering people in need and providing them with food, water and medical care. Volunteers also cleared trash from "layups," sites along the border where migrants rest and drop excess baggage to lighten their loads before continuing their journeys (fig. 1). As she watched bags of dirty clothing being tossed into the garbage, Ipsen wondered if something constructive could be done with the clothes instead, and hatched an idea to convert the discarded jeans, work shirts, bandanas and other discarded items into quilt-like textiles that could be inscribed with the names of deceased migrants. "We have got to use this material to show them what is going on in the desert," she said.[1]

Whether we call the people who leave their homes seeking better lives elsewhere illegal aliens, refugees, undocumented border crossers, immigrants or simply "migrants," migration is an international phenomenon that has been going on for as long as anyone can remember. From Biblical accounts of the Jews fleeing Egypt, to our ancestors who traveled across oceans for opportunities in America, to the influx of migration into Europe from war zones today, people always have been on the move in order to get someplace where they and their families could be more secure. In recent years, those journeying from Mexico and Central America to the United States have faced unnecessarily harsh dangers. According to the Colibri Center for Human Rights in Tucson, "Migration is as old as humanity itself. High rates of migrant death are not. Today we face a human rights crisis, as each year hundreds of migrants die along the U.S-Mexico border."[2]

Until the 1990s that border was relatively open, allowing workers to pass back and forth between jobs in the north and their families in the south, but the situation changed after 1994 when the North American Free Trade Agreement (NAFTA), created to expand trade between the United States, Canada and Mexico, went into effect.[3] NAFTA devastated local economies in Mexico by allowing the importation of cheap subsidized corn and other goods, putting farmers out of work by eliminating their markets.[4] Immigration to the United States—legal or not—jumped dramatically as Mexican and Central American people journeyed north to find jobs or to reunite with parents, children or spouses already living on this side of the border. United States policymakers realized that NAFTA would stimulate an influx in illegal immigration from Mexico and imposed strict border policies, sealing off traditional urban crossing areas with imposing steel walls and militarizing the border with over 20,000

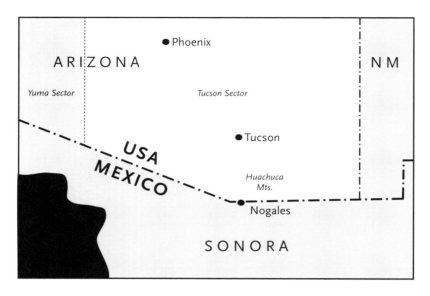

Fig. 2. Andy Mosier, map, Arizona-Sonora Borderlands. With permission from Margaret Regan, *Detained and Deported: Stories of Immigrant Families Under Fire* (Boston: Beacon Press, 2015).

Border Patrol agents by 2014.[5]

To avoid detection by agents, undocumented migrants began crossing the international boundary where there were no walls and few agents, which happened to be in the most brutal, remote areas of southern Arizona (fig. 2). It was thought that the area's difficulty would dissuade anyone from trying to cross there. Former Immigration and Naturalization Service Commissioner Doris Meissner admitted to the *Arizona Republic,* "We did believe that geography would be an ally to us . . . it was our sense that the number of people crossing the border through Arizona would go down to a trickle, once people realized what it's like."[6] People who are desperate cannot be deterred, however, and the result was an epidemic of deaths on the border due to the region's extreme heat and rough terrain, lack of water and distance from help. To make matters worse, drug cartels in northern Mexico control the activities of "coyotes," hired guides to whom migrants pay exorbitant fees to take them across the border. As coyotes usher groups of migrants through the desert, people can fall ill or be injured, and, rather than hold up the group and risk detection by the Border Patrol, sick travelers often are left behind to fend for themselves.

A United States Government Accountability Office report in 2006 showed a direct correlation between migrant deaths and United States government policies. According to the report's findings, there was a decline in migrant deaths along the southwestern United States border between 1990 and 1994, before the imposition of NAFTA and new border security policies, followed by an increase after those policies went into effect. Migrant deaths doubled from the mid-1990s through 2003, an increase attributed to a growing number of deaths in the Border Patrol's Tucson Sector, which runs along 262 miles of the international border and encompasses most of the state of Arizona, from the New Mexico state line to Yuma County.[7] The Tucson Sector is one of the busiest in the country in terms of migrant apprehensions and has the highest rates of migrant deaths in comparison to reported apprehensions.[8] The Pima County Office of the Medical Examiner in Tucson, which investigates ninety-five percent of the migrant deaths occurring in Arizona, examined 2,413 remains from 1990 to 2013. The office reported only five to twenty-one migrant deaths a year during the 1990s, but since 1999 they have investigated an average of 163 migrant deaths annually.[9] The deceased primarily have been men, but women's deaths more than doubled between 1998 and 2005.[10] Although migration slowed significantly after the global economic downturn in 2008, the rate of deaths to Border Patrol apprehensions actually increased exponentially, probably due to undocumented migrants traveling deeper into the desert to avoid detection, lengthening their journeys without sufficient food and water.[11] Sadly, a large number of the dead were unidentifiable either because they did not carry personal documents or their bodies were too decomposed by the time they were found. Their families never knew what had happened to them.[12]

Transforming Trash

In 2007, after her epiphany in the desert layup, Ipsen formed an organization called *Los Desconocidos,* Spanish for "the unknowns," in reference to the large percentage of deceased migrants who are never identified. *Los Desconocidos* had two interrelated goals: to document migrants' deaths in the Border Patrol's Tucson Sector with an annual memorial quilt and to increase public awareness of the deaths and why they are happening. Ipsen thought that a quilt would be a provocative object, "a good visual" for the cause. She was not a quilt maker, but she knew that quilts had been used in the past to raise consciousness about human rights abuses.[13]

Certainly the best-known quilt in the service of social change is the NAMES Project, often called simply "the AIDS Quilt," begun in 1985 by Cleve Jones when he created a panel in memory of his best friend who had died from the disease. In an *Uncoverings* paper, "A Text of the Times: The NAMES Project," Lawrence Howe discussed how the unique multi-panel quilt raised public awareness by revealing the names behind the AIDS statistics.[14] As the quilt grew in size, the disease progressively ravaged not only members of the gay community but others who were vulnerable. When it was dramatically displayed on the Mall in Washington, D.C., the gigantic quilt was viewed as both a remembrance of those who died and a collective political statement demanding a cure. The enormity of the quilt made it impossible to ignore the fact that thousands of quiet deaths were occurring unabated, while the personal stories embedded in the panels swayed public opinion from blaming the victims for getting sick, to feeling compassion for them.

Twenty years after the birth of the NAMES Project, Ipsen imagined a Migrant Quilt Project to reveal that thousands of unacknowledged deaths were happening in Southern Arizona. Ipsen invited individuals and organizations to make quilts for each year since 2000, when documentation of deceased migrants began. She believed that heartfelt, handmade quilts could be an effective means to honor those who died and to encourage people to support humane immigration reform. Her employment of quilts to influence popular opinion harkened back to the famous motto of nineteenth-century abolitionists regarding needlework expressing anti-slavery sentiments: "May the point of our needles prick the slave-owner's conscience."[15]

Ipsen and her fellow activists gathered textile items in the layups that could be used to make the Migrant Quilts. To be clear, they never collected materials near a death site, out of respect for the deceased person and to preserve the scene for the medical examiner. Much of what they salvaged was iconically American: denim blue jeans along with faded shirts and bandanas. Ipsen thoroughly washed the clothing and volunteers fashioned purses and tote bags from the jeans, calling them "Sonoran Sacks" and selling them to support start-up costs for *Los Desconocidos.*[16] Some of the more heart-wrenching items found in the layups were Mexican *bordados,* hand-embroidered cloths typically used to wrap tortillas. The juxtaposition of blue jeans and sentimental *bordados* in those sites was undeniable evidence of globalization, but their presence also humanized migrants. In an article about art made from migrants' discards,

Robert Neustadt observed, "Contemplating these hand-crafted cloths, embroidered with care, one recognizes that these so-called 'illegal alien criminals' are, in fact, people with dreams, people with families, people who love other people."[17]

Ipsen was not the first person to consider reusing migrants' cast-offs for creative purposes. Artists in Southern Arizona and beyond have been inspired by the untold stories and residual energy contained in items left behind in the desert. In the process of making art, they have transformed things that were seen as trash into icons of human suffering. Tucson photographer Michael Hyatt photographed objects he found along migrant trails for his book, *Migrant Artifacts: Magic and Loss in the Sonoran Desert,* a compelling photo essay witnessing to the dangers and tragedy of migrants' journeys.[18] Debbi McCullough has used personal items she found in the desert to create shrines, artist books, and scroll-like *Calendars of Death* listing migrants who died from 2010 to 2011. The calendar for July, the deadliest month, measured six inches wide by nine feet long.[19] Valarie James, who lives in a rural community where both migrant and Border Patrol presence are high, gathered discarded clothing, personal items and *bordados,* assembling them into evocative installation pieces that she exhibited locally and internationally to bring attention to migrant deaths.[20] James, McCullough, and two other artists collaborated to create three life-sized figures for an outdoor installation, *The Mothers; Las Madres/No More Tears; No Más Lágrimas.* They built one figure by layering a pulp made from migrants' jeans and desert plants over a precast body form, and covered two companion figures with burlap bags used to smuggle marijuana. The *Madres,* standing in a sculpture garden at a community college in Tucson, represent mothers affected by immigration: vulnerable migrating mothers and broken-hearted mothers at home waiting for word of their loved ones.[21]

Anthropologists interpret items left behind by migrants as cultural objects imbued with meaning about the people who owned them. A poster produced by the Colibri Center for Human Rights attempted to bring a human face to migrants. *The Things They Carried: A Memorial to Lives Lost on the Border* depicts more than 100 items recovered by the Pima County Medical Examiner's Office near the bodies of migrant men, women and children who died in Arizona between 2000 and 2009; sometimes, these objects are the only clues to help families identify the remains of their loved ones. The drawings of identification cards, photographs, asthma inhalers, birth control pills, religious images, rosaries, contact lens cases, underwear, books, cosmetics, stuffed animals, toothbrushes, eye-glasses, jewelry, playing cards, etc., prove that migrants are human beings like us.[22] At the University of Michigan, the Undocumented Migration Project (U.M.P.), led by Jason DeLeon, an assistant professor of anthropology, studies immigrants' discards from an archaeological perspective. DeLeon takes students on collecting treks in the borderlands of northern Mexico and Southern Arizona. In 2013, the University's Institute of Humanities displayed the objects gathered by the students in an exhibit, *State of Exception,* along with Robert Barnes' videography shot along the border fence, in an effort to inspire new conversations and ways of thinking about immigration policy.[23]

Birth of the Migrant Quilt Project

When someone agrees to make a Migrant Quilt, Ipsen assigns the quilt-maker or group a list of deceased migrants' names from a specific federal fiscal year, which runs from October 1 until September 30. As an agency of the United States Homeland Security Department, the Border Patrol uses the federal fiscal year to count migrant statistics, and Ipsen thought it apt for the quilts to do so as well. She obtains the lists of names from the organization *Derechos Humanos* (meaning "human rights"), which compiles them from the Pima County Office of the Medical Examiner's data. Ipsen provides migrant jeans and other cloth items to use as the primary material for the quilts, but quiltmakers supply the foundation or backing fabric and anything else they need to finish their quilts. They are free to design their quilts according to their own inspiration and can employ any fiber art techniques they like to create the quilts, but must conform to a few basic rules. Each quilt is to be inscribed with the names of every decedent on the fiscal year's list, with unidentified migrants indicated as *"Desconocido"* or "Unknown." The words "Tucson Sector" and the quilt's date range are to be written at the top of the quilt. Upon completion, quilt-makers agree to give their quilts to *Los Desconocidos.*

The first Migrant Quilt was made by Project Amor, a Tucson non-profit organization serving low-income Spanish-speaking families of children with disabilities and literacy needs. The quilt, documenting migrant deaths from October 1, 2003 to September 30, 2004, was made by Project Amor's staff members along with adults and children receiving services from the organization (fig. 3). Participants wrote migrants' names or *"Desconocido"* on four-inch denim patches cut from blue jeans. Despite the

Fig. 3. Project Amor, *2003–2004 Migrant Quilt*, 2008. Canvas and denim with paint and mixed media. 91 1/2 x 55 1/2 inches. Wilson Graham Photography.

morbidity of their task, they used colorful dimensional fabric pens to write the names and painted often-whimsical motifs on the patches, such as hearts, flowers, stars, rosaries, crosses, hands, and even a drawing of a baseball. They applied ribbons and bows, small pom-poms, rickrack and buttons to some of the squares. Staff members assembled the huge "quilt" by gluing the patches onto a bright red canvas panel, and covered the patches' raw edges with red braid. At the top, they painted "Tucson Sector" and "2003–2004" and installed grommets to facilitate hanging the quilt.

Admittedly, it stretches the definition of the term to call this textile creation a quilt. There is no fabric sandwich, no batting, and the only place it was stitched was to sew a channel for a stick at the bottom to help the canvas lie flat. It is a quilt in spirit, however, assembled from fabric cut into squares and arranged in a grid format. Furthermore, it was deliberately modeled on earlier social justice quilts, especially the NAMES Project quilt, and was intended to inspire compassion in the hearts of those who viewed it. With the completion of this quilt, the Migrant Quilt Project was official and Ipsen had a visual. She loaded photos of the brightly-colored work on the *Los Desconocidos* website and printed its images on a flyer to recruit people to make additional quilts.

The second quilt came about as the result of a personal invitation to Suzanne Hesh, a Tucson immigration activist who moved in the same circles as Ipsen. A contemporary textile artist and retired art teacher, Hesh had been involved with fabric, needles and thread since childhood. In the 1980s, she was intrigued with making art quilts, which allowed her to combine fabric with her design impulse. When migrant deaths in Southern Arizona became a major crisis, she founded a border and immigration ministry at her church and began writing a biweekly emailed newsletter listing opportunities for involvement and study. Her passion for teaching others about the immigration crisis is an expression of her belief that everyone is the same in the eyes of God. She stated, "We all deserve equal opportunity to live in dignity, fulfill our destinies, take care of our families, live with respect and be respected."[24]

Hesh has produced over a dozen textile artworks expressing her compassion for migrants who die needlessly and tragically. She stitched *Memorial for Fourteen* in honor of fourteen migrants who died in an auto accident in southern Arizona in 2001. On *Los Desconocidos,* she hand-embroidered the words "*los desconocidos*" line after line, in beige thread on beige linen, the words becoming fainter with each repetition until they

Fig. 4. Project Amor, *2003–2004 Migrant Quilt*, 2008. Canvas and denim with paint and mixed media. 91 1/2 x 55 1/2 inches. Wilson Graham Photography.

completely disappeared. *Leyvanta la voz (Raise your voice)* was based on a nine-patch quilt block, each square illustrating an aspect of the flight of migrants (fig. 4). On the label for an exhibit in Tucson, she wrote: "It commemorates all people in migration, especially those who travel South to North. For thousands, their movement, identity and lives are lost in the desert, in the land a few minutes or miles from where you are reading this."[25] Hesh has been active in the international *Fuentes Rojas* (Red Fountains) movement to raise visibility for victims of the violent drug wars in Mexico, hand stitching police reports about victims' deaths in red thread on men's white handkerchiefs.[26] Her art and border activism are integrated, flowing back and forth in her life. "Art is always a natural expression of social issues," she explains. Not surprisingly, Hesh was receptive to Ipsen's request to create a Migrant Quilt, which would give her another opportunity to express her feelings about "avoidable death an hour's drive from where I live. How could I not respond to that?"[27]

In addition to being the author of this paper, I am an artist and a quiltmaker and have been in an art group with Hesh for many years. At a meeting in early 2010 she told us about the Migrant Quilt Project and invited group members to collaborate with her to make a quilt. Alice Vinson, then an art graduate student, agreed, and so did I, wanting to expand my horizons after retiring that spring from my career as an art curator. Our quilt would document the names of 205 individuals, a large portion with unknown identities, whose bodies were recovered during the 2005–2006 fiscal year. We met to brainstorm design layouts, and settled on a scrappy arrangement of patches cut from the clothing and *bordados* that Ipsen gave us. We wanted the effect to be raw and rustic, similar to the materials themselves and the conditions in which they were salvaged.

Our project "got real" when we dumped out the bags of clothing and sorted the items between us. I have collected and worked with fabric for many years, and had even stitched a blue jean quilt for my son in the 1980s, but with this project I encountered cloth in a completely different context. In contrast to the yard goods from which I usually make quilts, the faded jeans, sun-bleached shirts, and threadbare bandanas seemed as if they still held the energy and pain of the people who had worn them. Although we realized that they were not from dead bodies, it was overwhelming to handle such intimate items belonging to strangers who had been through harrowing journeys. Then Vinson started to cry as she held up a tiny pair of twelve-month-sized denim overalls. Ipsen did not anticipate the emotional responses to working with the clothing and was surprised by how moving the experience has been for her and the quiltmakers. "We are making the quilts out of migrants' clothing, so you get this hands-on, tactile feel of a life that crossed out there."[28]

Reading the spreadsheet with the names of the deceased migrants for our quilt was emotionally fraught as well. A cold official document, it listed the victims' names or the word "Unknown" chronologically according to the dates their remains were discovered. Additional columns indicated the decedents' sex, age, country of origin, geographic coordinates for where they were discovered, and cause of death, which most often was

Fig. 5. Peggy Hazard, Suzanne Hesh, & Alice Vinson, *2005–2006 Migrant Quilt*, 2010. Canvas and denim jeans with shirts, bandanas, embroideries, cloth and paint. 86 1/2 x 60 inches. Wilson Graham Photography.

hyperthermia or exposure, but also included blunt force injuries, auto accidents, homicide, hanging, and undetermined reasons. This was more information than we had expected and at that point we lost whatever naïveté we still held onto about migrants' experiences. In contrast to the grim data in the listings, the people's long, lyrical names felt like poetry to read aloud: "Gloria de Quintanilla, Benito Acevado Castañeda, Stephany del Toro Hernández."

We divided the names between us and devised our own techniques for inscribing them onto mostly rectangular patches we cut from the clothes (fig. 5). Hesh machine-embroidered free-motion cursive text in big, looping letters to write names on pieces of denim, a man's shirt collar, and the back pockets of jeans. Vinson, who enjoys slow handwork, claimed the soft plaid men's shirts and used a reverse appliqué technique to create windows in her patches, framing names she had computer-printed on white fabric. I have a devotion to the Virgin of Guadalupe, the patroness of Mexico whose image often accompanies migrants on their journeys in the belief that she will deliver them safely. So that she would have a presence on the quilt, each of my patches contained a small printed picture of the Virgin beside the migrant's name or the word "unknown" computer-printed in red letters on white fabric.

The three of us met again to pin our patches to a large piece of cotton canvas tacked on my studio wall, intentionally leaving the side edges of the quilt ragged. I filled in blank spaces with leftover scraps of the clothing, big flowers cut from *bordados,* and snippets of red printed fabric, then machine-stitched all the elements to the canvas. Hesh created a bright gold banner for the top and painted "Tucson Border Sector" and "10/2005 −9/2006" on it in large script, attached red and white flowers from *bordados,* made a label for the back, and installed grommets for hanging. Then we gave the quilt to Ipsen.

Unbeknownst to us, "our quilt" was displayed at an event in Tucson a few weeks later, and an acquaintance who saw it contacted me to express how much she liked it. Her positive comments made me proud of our accomplishment, knowing that the quilt was having its intended effect to honor migrants who had died, and make a public statement about their deaths. Ipsen lent the quilt to a border conference in Maryland where it represented in words and image the disaster taking place in southern Arizona.

Ipsen continued to show the quilts locally, including at a Peace Fair in Tucson and at annual Border Issues Fairs held at a church in Sahuarita, south of Tucson. Shura Wallin, co-founder of the Green Valley/Sahuarita Samaritans, saw the Migrant Quilts at the fairs for many years and considers them powerful objects. "Every scrap of fabric had a dream behind it," she said, "and every name had a dream, and those dreams died in the desert."[29]

Ipsen observed that, like the artists who made the quilts, viewers also are affected emotionally. "People get very weepy," she commented. "They don't understand the broad spectrum of the whole thing, and this is a visual that people can see and grasp and come to understand." The sheer magnitude of the quilts communicates their message: the huge size, the incomprehensible number of names on them, and the large percentages of unidentified deaths. "It challenges one's belief to see as many as 200 names on a quilt and one-third to one-half are unidentified. Their families don't have closure, they don't have a body to mourn."[30]

When cultures collide, as they do in the borderlands, issues can get complicated and be difficult to sort out; naturally, not everyone who views the Migrants Quilts is sympathetic to their purpose. When Ipsen displayed the quilts at an artists' open studio weekend in a mountain town north of Tucson, the response by a group of women from a nearby retirement community was to tell Ipsen that the migrants had broken the law and their deaths were not "our" problem.[31] While it is true that the names documented on the quilts represent people who acted illegally, the point of making and exhibiting them is to reveal the deceased migrants' relationship to us as fellow human beings whose lives deserve to be acknowledged and whose deaths should have been prevented.

In October 2012, the author included two Migrant Quilts in an exhibit, *Quilts Making a Difference,* at the Tucson Meet Yourself festival. The popular annual folk life event was founded by folklorist Dr. James Griffith, whose life's work has been the interpretation of the people and customs on the borderlands where Southern Arizona and northern Sonora, Mexico, intersect. The exhibit featured quilts used in Arizona to raise consciousness and support social issues and needs, such as a World War I-era Red Cross fundraising quilt and quilts auctioned by Quilt for a Cause to support breast cancer screening and treatment, as well as quilts made to commemorate the women's vote and to express grief after the 9/11 attack and the 2011 Tucson shooting.[32]

It was exciting to show the Migrant Quilts in the context of other consciousness-raising quilts, adjacent to a display of quilts from the Southern Arizona AIDS Foundation memorializing community members who died from AIDS, and near a lawn where panels from the NAMES Project were ritually unfolded in a ceremony. The Migrant Quilts' dramatic scale and brilliant colors seemed to draw festival visitors into the exhibit space, but people tended to grow quiet when they looked closer and realized that the quilts were constructed from migrants' clothing and recorded the names of fellow human beings who perished only miles away from where they stood.

Ipsen set up a workspace at the exhibit where festival-goers could decorate *"Desconocido"* name patches for a future quilt. Laraine Daly Jones, Collections Manager at the Arizona Historical Society, visited for a few hours one afternoon, embroidering denim squares. Reflecting on that day, she said,

> I was moved to tears when I first saw the memorial quilts made as part of the Migrant Quilt Project. So many people who succumbed to the unflagging, unbearable desert heat, and many of them are known only as Los Desconocidos, their given names lost. Somewhere loved ones worry and pray for them, wondering what has happened to them, and they will probably never know. I am grateful that there are quilters who have found a way to remember them, so that their lives do not end without meaning.[33]

One day during the festival, Tucson artist Jennifer Eschedor viewed the quilt exhibit. "Before I knew it, I had struck up a conversation with Jody [Ipsen], and she was so welcoming," Eschedor recalled. "It unfolded for me that day."[34] Eschedor decided she "was in" and agreed to make a Migrant Quilt. Although she was aware that her friends, Hesh, Vinson and this author had made one, "the concept of it was not of any personal concern until I started to realize just how many deaths were involved, and hearing about Jody's first-hand experiences. That, to me, really drove it home." Receiving the salvaged clothing had a big impact on her: "When Jody first gave me the clothing in a paper bag it was packed with such emotion. We had talked so much about the deaths that they were loaded objects."

Eschedor majored in textiles at Kent State University but quiltmaking was not in the academic curriculum. "It was that whole art versus craft argument," she explained.[35] She got involved with quilts later, when her mother retired and the two of them explored quiltmaking as a shared activity. It became a passion; her mom joined a group, and Eschedor discovered friends with whom she made safety-themed wall quilts for a women's shelter. Looking back, she realized that the shelter pieces were her first experience with socially-conscious quilts. "Power can be so misused," she explained. "With the migrants, we are talking about government intervention, but with abused women we're talking about . . . where power is being misused within relationships." Associations between relationships in the insect and human worlds have been a recurring theme in Eschedor's art, which she has expressed with pictures of beetles, human skulls and skeletons printed from hand-cut linoleum blocks. Incorporating Mexican *Día de los Muertos* imagery in her work has helped Eschedor explore her feelings about death.

Although Eschedor included lino-printed skulls on her Migrant Quilt documenting 2011–2012, she did not associate the quilt with her personal art because the primary purpose for making a Migrant Quilt was to get the names out (fig. 6). She exercised artistic license with the quilt, nevertheless. "I really wanted it to seem sort of beat up, to represent the brutality that they had experienced. So rather than appliqué the names on the top, I tore the denim to reveal the names underneath. That process conveyed more suffering."[36] She deliberately chose pieces of clothing "that were clearly worn or stained because they had more energy . . . and I could imagine the person who wore them." She stitched in pieces of dark blue bandanas and a baseball cap with the Virgin of Guadalupe embroidered on it, "because it represents the importance of religion in day-to-day life for many of the migrants."[37]

This quilt featured three intact *bordados* that Ipsen found in layup sites. One, stitched with a spray of red flowers, spelled out the Spanish words *"Duerme amor mio,"* which translates to "Sleep, my love," while on a second cloth embroidered leaves and flowers framed the text *"Contigo en la distancia,"* meaning "With you from a distance."[38] Considering that the cloths ended up in a lonely Arizona canyon, the sentiments sewn onto them were poignant. Had the mothers or sweethearts who made the cloths folded warm tortillas inside before stashing them in their loved ones' backpacks? In her heart, Eschedor believed that the women who stitched the *bordados* had lost their loved ones to the harsh desert.[39]

Two years later, when Eschedor made a second Migrant Quilt repre-

Fig. 6. Jennifer Eschedor, *2011–2012 Migrant Quilt*, 2012. Denim jeans and cloth with bandanas, hat, milagros, embroideries and mixed media. 46 1/2 x 52 inches. Wilson Graham Photography.

senting 2012–2013, she decided that the skull image would have a stronger impact when repeated many times. (fig 7) "I really wanted the skull to be used as a sign of death. Nothing cutesy; I didn't want it to be like *Día de los Muertos* in any way; I just wanted it to be *dead*."[40]

Expressions of Grief

In a 2010 *Uncoverings* paper, "Wrapped in Meanings: Quilts for Families of Soldiers Killed in the Afghanistan and Iraq Wars," Jonathan Gregory described patriotic quilts made to comfort the families of U.S. servicemen who died in the line of duty. His description of the quiltmakers' motivations to "do something" about the war's suffering, placing the names of the dead on the quilts, and using symbols and text thought to be mean-

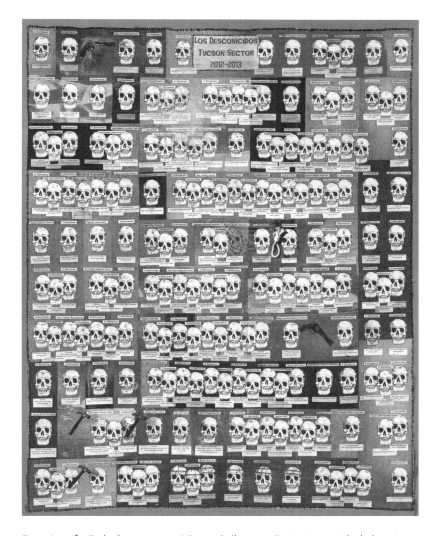

Fig. 7. Jennifer Eschedor, *2012–2013 Migrant Quilt,* 2014. Denim jeans with cloth, paint and mixed media. 69 1/2 x 56 inches. Wilson Graham Photography.

ingful to the servicemen's families, parallels the intent, process, and signif-icance of the Migrant Quilts.[41] Likewise, Carolyn H. Krone and Thomas M. Horner's paper, "Her Grief in the Quilt," described the therapeutic value of quiltmaking as an activity to heal those who are grieving and also documented the practice of incorporating loved ones' clothing in memorial quilts.[42] Intimate objects, especially clothes that have been worn next to the body of the deceased, can be a comfort for survivors, and NAMES panels often have included clothing and personal items for this reason.[43] The decision to make the Migrants Quilts from discarded migrants' clothing was highly symbolic and the quiltmakers felt it restored dignity to those doomed people. Although the clothes in the Migrant Quilts do not come from death sites, it is difficult for viewers to avoid associating the fabric with the individuals whose names are on the quilt. "If you at all are sensitive or aware," said Suzanne Hesh, "you can assume that the people who wore the clothing went through a horrific experience."[44]

Cornelia Bayley is an energetic quiltmaker who lives in Green Valley, a retirement community south of Tucson, and has seen the migrant crisis play out almost literally in her backyard. When hiking in nearby hills, she has come across discarded migrant backpacks, rotting socks, and disintegrating water bottles. She was aware of the humanitarian tragedy before moving to Arizona in 2012 and has friends who are members of the Samaritans, but as much as she wished she could ride out into the desert to assist migrants, it was not something she could do. She found a good way to serve the cause when she encountered Ipsen and a display of Migrant Quilts at a Border Issues Fair in Sahuarita.

Bayley has made quilts since her college days at Berkeley in the late 1960s. "I almost never haven't quilted," she said, but she did not like to work with quilt patterns, preferring more free-form, forgivable techniques such as log cabins and strip piecing.[45] She sewed a number of autobiographical quilts when going through tough times, such as a house-themed quilt she made when she feared she would lose her house after her divorce. Whenever someone close to her died, she made a quilt "to work out the pain, get through the hard part."[46]

In her enthusiasm for the Migrant Quilt Project, Bayley made two quilts in a single year, but found it difficult to begin the first one, recording the deaths from 2010−2010, because reading the names of the migrants was so distressing (fig. 8). "I was very upset by it," she said; "I cried."[47] In fact, she cried so profusely while embroidering names on the faded denim patches that her red cotton thread ran. She realized that the bleeding symbolized her sadness and thereafter deliberately wetted the thread so that it would run to create an impression of tears on the quilt. Near the upper right corner, beneath the Virgin of Guadalupe, she wrote the words *Con Nuestras Lágrimas* and its translation, "With Our Tears," and surrounded the text with a rosary.

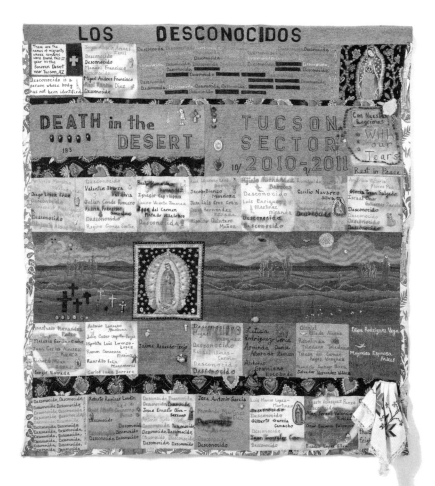

Fig. 8. Cornelia Bayley, *2010–2011 Migrant Quilt,* 2014. Denim jeans and cloth with embroideries, beads, milagros, crosses and mixed media. 61 x 54 1/2 inches. Wilson Graham Photography.

Bayley sewed a wide swath of landscape-printed upholstery fabric across the center of the quilt and accented the scene with stitchery and embellishments. She embroidered the moon and stars on the left side of the sky, and the sun on the right, giving the sense of a day and night passing, evoking the experience of migrants trudging through the desert day after day. She stitched hills, mountains, saguaro cacti, and flowers, and created a cemetery of crosses. The Virgin of Guadalupe appeared twice on the quilt, along with coffin and skeleton-shaped beads, buttons, and *milagros*.[48] On the lower right, Bayley draped a *bordado* over a patch embroidered with the questions, "Did you see a bird the day you died? Were you hot, thirsty, and frightened?"

Bayley's second quilt, for 2001–2002, put death squarely in the viewer's face (fig. 9). It featured a landscape cut from a quilting fabric that depicts saguaros silhouetted against a stunning orange sunset. The classic Arizona backdrop was not used here as a pretty postcard image or an office of tourism advertisement, but as the setting for death. She wrote "Lost Dreams, Lost Hopes, Lost Loves, Lost Lives" across the sky and on the ground below. This quilt included less migrant clothing and more fabric from Bayley's eclectic stash. "I use fabrics with Mexican themes,

Fig. 9. Cornelia Bayley, *2001–2002 Migrant Quilt,* 2014. Denim jeans and cloth with beads, milagros and mixed media. 89 1/2 x 47 inches. Wilson Graham Photography.

Mexican *milagros,* and other religious artifacts that have cultural origins in Mexico, Guatemala, Honduras, and other places where these travelers started their perilous journey, leaving behind their families, full of hopes and dreams for their future."[49]

Some people wear their hearts on their sleeves, but Bayley wears hers on her quilts. The Migrant Quilt Project dovetailed with her values and world view. "I've always been very progressive. I've made political quilts, anti-war quilts, so this was just a natural."[50] She was honored to help share the message about how many people have died in the desert. "You can't live here without thinking about those people, and we know the brutality of the desert. So there wasn't any way I could not do something." The same year that she made the Migrant Quilts, Bayley sewed a quilt to comfort a Tucson woman, Rosa Robles Loreto, who took sanctuary at Southside Presbyterian Church to avoid deportation and keep her family intact. Bayley has attended hearings for Operation Streamline, a "zero tolerance" border enforcement program that drastically increased immigration prosecutions and forced undocumented migrants through the federal criminal justice system and into United States prisons. "That's another thing I am thinking of making a quilt on," she shared with the author. "It broke my heart."[51]

Nancy Amann is a self-proclaimed "snowbird" from Maryland, who spends her winters in Tucson. Like Bayley, she tried to volunteer with the Samaritans but it was not right for her, and when she met Ipsen at a Border Fair and viewed the Migrant Quilts, she saw that as her way to be involved.[52] Amann helped Ipsen complete the Migrant Quilt for 2007–2008 from patches made a few years earlier by high school students in Douglas, a border town in southeastern Arizona (fig. 10). Library aides and students in Spanish language classes stitched the names with beautiful embroidery or wrote them with fabric paints, sometimes in a graffiti-like style. They embellished patches with buttons, fringe, braid and painted cactus, crosses and skulls. Amann completed the name patches and made all of the *desconocido* patches, which on this quilt far outnumbered the named ones.

One patch that Amann made incorporated a poignant photograph of Josseline Quinteros, a fourteen-year-old girl immortalized in *Death of Josseline,* an insightful book about the human side of the immigration crisis by Tucson author Margaret Regan.[53] In January 2008, Josseline and her younger brother were traveling with a group from their town in El Salvador, on their way to San Diego to be reunited with their mother,

Fig. 10. Douglas High School & Nancy Amann, *2007–2008 Migrant Quilt,* 2014. Bed sheet and denim jeans with cloth, paint, bandana, ribbon and mixed media. 83 x 69 1/2 inches. Wilson Graham Photography.

when Josseline became sick and could not continue. The group's coyote left her behind, assuring the teenager that the Border Patrol would find her, but that did not happen. Josseline had only the clothes she was wearing for protection from below-freezing nighttime temperatures, and she died alone in the Arizona borderlands. Three weeks later, a volunteer on patrol found her body after spotting her bright green tennis shoes in the desert.

As the quilt's centerpiece, Amann used a bandana Ipsen had found in a child's abandoned backpack, depicting the Virgin of Guadalupe flanked by flags of the United States and Mexico. An eighty-eight-year-old friend quilted the bandana onto a tan-colored sheet, and Nancy arranged the name and *desconocido* patches around it. To emphasize the meaning of the quilt, she placed patches below "Tucson Sector" containing the words "Broken Hearts/Broken Dreams/Broken Promises" and "The detritus/of the/Sonoran Desert." Still not finished, she "wanted people to know the ages and cause of death to make their deaths more real," so she created "prayer flags" from red ribbons, wrote the death information on them, and stitched the flags along the bottom and two sides of the quilt. Amann said:

> I'm not a terrific quilter, just enthusiastic about the project. My hope was that anyone viewing the quilt would realize how many bodies weren't found in time to identify them. All the parents, children, grandparents, lovers . . . who had no idea what happened to those people. I want people to understand that no matter how they feel about the problems of illegal immigration, the migrants are people. Like you and me.[54]

Verni Greenfield took an interesting approach for her 2009–2010 quilt by writing the names of the deceased migrants on the red and white stripes of a United States flag that she sewed onto a blanket found in a layup (fig. 11). In the field of blue where fifty stars usually lie, she designed a nighttime landscape depicting an empty road heading toward hills on the horizon, with a scattering of stars in the sky. Using such a politically-charged symbol as the American flag was a bold decision and effectively illustrated where the migrants were headed. Greenfield stated that working with the materials felt like a "sacred act" and that the quilt's humble materials "reflect the sacrifice and embody the remnants of deceased immigrants' dreams and hopes of a new life in 'El Norte.'"[55] She wanted her quilt to remind those who are Americans by birth not to take their citizenship for granted. "Most Americans never need to sacrifice for freedom and opportunity and may misunderstand or feel threatened by those who strive to join them."

Fig. 11. Verni Greenfield, *2009–2010 Migrant Quilt,* 2011. United States flag and cloth with paint and sequins. 62 x 67 inches. Wilson Graham Photography.

Human Rights on the Border

In 1994, the year that NAFTA was established, Consueulo Underwood, a Mexican American artist who taught at San Jose State University, created *Virgen de los Caminos (Virgin of the Roads)* to represent the struggle of Mexican people who, as she and her parents had, come to the U.S. hoping to give their families better lives (fig. 12). She embroidered the Virgin of Guadalupe in the center of the quilt and stitched flowers resembling those on Mexican *bordados* on the four sides and corners. The quilt's charm ends there; embroidered barbed wire crisscrosses the width of the quilt, signifying the separation of people and opportunity at the international boundary, and the Virgin's face is a hollow-eyed skull. The barely-visible white quilting stitches repeatedly spell the word "caution" and trace the

Fig. 12. Consuelo Jiménez Underwood, *Virgen de los Caminos,* 1994. Embroidered and quilted cotton and silk with graphite. 58 x 36 inches. Smithsonian American Art Museum 1996.77, Museum purchase.

outlined silhouette of a fleeing family, a symbol used on highway warning signs in the U.S. border states to alert drivers to watch for people on foot.[56]

Los hilos de la vida (The Threads of Life) was a cooperative quilting group that evolved out of a parenting and family literacy class for Spanish-speaking women in Mendocino County, California. From 2005 to 2010, women in the group designed and sewed appliquéd story quilts depicting their families' illegal migration experiences, as well as dreams, memories and often-painful personal stories. In the process of making their quilts, they learned to express themselves visually and, in speaking about the quilts, they improved their verbal skills as well.[57] Angeles Segura's emotionally-moving quilt, *The Great Risk,* illustrated her family's fatal journey across the border into the saguaro-studded Arizona desert, during which her mother died. *Death Lives in the Desert* by Luz Maria Bucio, portrays the dangers endured by migrants: jumping the line, hiding behind rocks, children dying from lack of food and water, and capture by Border Patrol agents (fig. 13).[58] During the years that the group was active, their quilts were widely visible in exhibits and in print, including a book that the cooperative published.[59] The quilts were exhibited in northern California, and at the National Museum of Mexican Art in Chicago, the American Visionary Art Museum in Baltimore, and the Pacific International Quilt Festival. Karen Musgrave interviewed thirty-eight members of the group for the Quilt Alliance's Save Our Stories Project.[60] In contrast to the Migrant Quilts made by sympathetic outsiders who are concerned about migrant deaths as a human rights cause, the quilts sewn by these women and by Underwood depict their own personal experiences with the border, migration and death.

In 2008, the Michigan State University Museum presented an exhibit called *Quilts and Human Rights* that included a compelling quilt, *Strange Fruit: A Century of Lynching and Murder 1865–1965.*[61] Made by April Shipp of Auburn Hills, Michigan, to document the names of lynching victims in the United States, it bears a striking resemblance to the Migrant Quilts, with its long list of people who died. Shipp was inspired to make her quilt after viewing a disturbing photograph in a book showing a woman lynched alongside her son and hanging from a bridge.[62] She sewed the quilt from a variety of fabrics in shades of mourning black and machine-embroidered the names with a rich gold Sulky thread to indicate her belief that everyone was precious in the eyes of God. She stated, "I did this Quilt in loving memory of my people, people I have never met, people whose names are not only woven into the fabric of this Quilt but also into the

Fig. 13. Luz Maria Bucio, Death Lives in the Desert, 2006. Quilted cloth with tulle and mixed media. 33 x 38 inches. Collection of Karen Musgrave.

fabric of my heart."[63] *Strange Fruit* is Shipp's attempt to reveal and emphasize the scale of an injustice that was ignored or unknown to the wider public. The hundreds of names embroidered on the lynching quilt, like the hundreds inscribed on the Migrant Quilts, serve as a monument to the memory of Shipp's people, a textile equivalent to the war memorials erected around the world to express communal grief and preserve the names of the dead for posterity.

These relatively recent quilts dealing with border issues and racism are contemporary manifestations of the human rights quilts made by nineteenth- and early-twentieth-century women. As Ferrero, Hedges, and Silber demonstrated in their landmark 1987 book, *Hearts and Hands: The Influence of Women and Quilts on American Society,* women stitched quilts to raise money and consciousness about the abolitionist cause and female suffrage, to support Civil War soldiers, and to show their alliance with the Temperance movement. In the decades since *Hearts and Hands* made its mark on quilt history scholarship, several *Uncoverings* papers have documented further examples of the places where quiltmaking converged with social and political matters, from a paper about quilts supporting President McKinley's campaign, to a dramatic story of justice being served when a quilt made by women prisoners proved that they had been unfairly charged with their crimes.[64] These papers, and others referred to earlier in this work, described how quilts communicated what their makers did not have the ability to articulate with their voices or their vote.

Quilts and Human Rights, published this year and based on the 2008 Michigan State University exhibit, continues the discussion of humanitarian quiltmaking addressed in *Hearts and Hands.* The book by Beth Donaldson, Marsha McDowell, Lynn Swanson and Mary Worrall surveys quilts used to "demonstrate solidarity with movements dedicated to advancing international human rights . . . to provide vehicles for the expression of feelings and memories about human rights violations, and to engage individuals in actions that will solve human rights issues."[65] One of the Migrant Quilts can be viewed in a section exploring how quilt projects in the late twentieth and early twenty-first century addressed issues related to "race, ethnicity, women's rights, gender, worker's culture, disabilities rights, and involvement in war."[66] The authors of *Quilts and Human Rights* also direct and coordinate the Quilt Index, the growing online database and public resource on quilts and quilt history. To increase the usefulness of the Quilt Index, they created thematic galleries, including one for "Human Rights Quilts" where documented Migrant Quilts will be cross-referenced, and they are working to document all the NAMES panels from the AIDS Memorial Quilt, to provide an interactive site for researchers and the loved ones of AIDS victims.

Compassion and Culture

A Haitian proverb says, "What the eye doesn't see, doesn't move the heart." The makers of the Migrant Quilts used discarded clothing, needles and thread to express their solidarity with migrants as fellow human beings.[67] When the quilts are displayed, people can see in them the clear and visible evidence of out-of-control migrant deaths taking place in southern Arizona. The quiltmakers hope that viewers feel compassion for the victims and are stirred to support policy change to eliminate the deaths. At the time this paper was written, eleven quilts were completed and three were in process, bringing the project up to date with a quilt representing every federal fiscal year since 2001–2002. Ipsen envisions that the Migrant Quilt Project will continue creating annual quilts "until the last person passes away in the desert, which could be centuries from now. We don't know."[68]

Anthropologist Robin Reineke, Director of the Colibri Center for Human Rights, has been involved closely with the crisis of migrant deaths on the border. A co-founder of the Missing Migrant Project, since 2006 she has worked to connect unidentified migrants' remains with their families. She views the Migrant Quilt Project as an artistic expression that actively mourns the loss of life in an environment where the deaths have become commonplace and that blames migrants for their own deaths:

> This casual acceptance of the near daily loss of life in the south-western U.S. is harmful not only to migrants and their families, but to the social wellbeing of our entire society. Only through grief, through public and political mourning, will we be able to collectively declare that these lives matter. From there, we can assert that their deaths are an unacceptable result of U.S. border policy. But first, they must be recognized as lives worth grieving. The Migrant Quilt Project is an act of care that reclaims these losses as our losses, and for that reason, is critically important.[69]

Ipsen sees the Migrant Quilt Project as "a permanent documentation of those lives lost and for what reasons and policies."[70] In order to preserve the quilts, they will be offered eventually to a history or anthropology museum that collects artifacts for the interpretation and study of border and immigration issues. While the quilts are valuable material culture objects representing a critical period in the histories of the United States and Mexico, ultimately, their makers feel that the importance of the Migrant Quilt Project will lie in its ability to play a role in inspiring a transformation of social and political consciousness.

Notes and References

1. Jody Ipsen, interviewed by author, March 20, 2015.
2. The Colibri Center for Human Rights, Fact Sheet, www.colibricenter.org/wp-content/uploads/2013/09/Fact-Sheet_Edited.pdf, 2014.
3. Office of the United States Trade Representative, Executive Office of the President, *North American Free Trade Agreement (NAFTA)*, ustr.gov/trade-agreements/free-trade-agreements/north-american-free-trade-agreement-nafta.
4. Daniel E. Martinez, Robin C. Reineke, Raquel Rubio-Goldsmith, and Bruce O. Parks, "Structural Violence and Migrant Deaths in Southern Arizona: Data from the Pima County Office of the Medical Examiner, 1990–2013," Journal on Migration and Human

Security 2, no. 4 (2014): 260.

5. Department of Homeland Security, Customs and Border Protection, www.cbp.gov/newsroom/stats/typical-day-fy2014.

6. Arizona Republic, August 10, 2000, in Raquel Rubio-Goldsmith, M. Melissa McCormick, Daniel Martinez, and Inez Magdalena Duarte, The "Funnel Effect" & Recovered Bodies of Unauthorized Migrants Processed by the Pima County Office of the Medical Examiner, 1990–2005, Report Submitted to the Pima County Board of Supervisors, The Binational Migration Institute, University of Arizona, 2006, 5.

7. United States Government Accountability Office, Illegal Immigration: Border-Crossing Deaths Have Doubled Since 1995; Border Patrol's Efforts to Prevent Deaths Have Not Been Fully Evaluated, Report to the Honorable Bill Frist, Majority Leader, U.S. Senate, GAO-06-770, August 2006,14.

8. United States Border Patrol Sector Profile, Fiscal Year 2014 (Oct. 1st through Sept. 30th), www.cbp.gov/sites/default/files/documents/USBP%20Stats%20FY2014%20sector%20profile.pdf.

9. Martinez, et al., "Structural Violence and Migrant Deaths in Southern Arizona," 267.

10. United States Government Accounting Office, Illegal Immigration: Border-Crossing Deaths Have Doubled Since 1995, 24–25.

11. The Binational Migration Institute, A Continued Humanitarian Crisis at the Border: Undocumented Border Crosser Deaths Recorded by the Pima County Office of the Medical Examiner, 1990–2012, The University of Arizona, June 2013, 27.

12. Brady McCombs, "Nearly 1,700 bodies, each one a mystery," Arizona Daily Star (Tucson), August 22, 2010.

13. Jody Ipsen interview.

14. Lawrence Howe, "A Text of the Times: The NAMES Project," in Uncoverings 12, ed. Laurel Horton (San Franciso, CA: American Quilt Study Group, 1991), 11–31.

15. Pat Ferrero, Hearts and Hands: The Influence of Women and Quilts on American Society (San Francisco, CA: The Quilt Digest Press, 1987), 72.

16. Jody Ipsen interview.

17. Robert Neustadt, "Art Created From Undocumented Immigrants' Discarded Objects," Utne Reader, (September/October 2013): 1.

18. Michael Hyatt, Migrant Artifacts: Magic and Loss in the Sonoran Desert (Los Angeles: Great Circle Books, 2007).

19. "Where Hope Goes to Die—An American Desert by Deborah McCullough," When Women Waken: A Journal of Poetry, Prose and Images by Women, November 30, 2013, www.whenwomenwaken.org/where-hope-goes-to-die-an-american-desert-by-deborah-mccullough.

20. Margaret Regan, "Tales From the Outskirts: Amado, Amado's Valarie James turns items left behind by migrants into compelling art," Tucson Weekly, July 22, 2010.

21. Sally Curd, "Las Madres Depict Migrants' Journeys," Aztec Press (Tucson), November 23, 2010 and Robert Neustadt, "Art Created," 3.

22. The Things They Carried: A Memorial to Lives Lost on the Border, Colibri Center for Human Rights; colibricenter.org/things-carried.

23. "Following the Footsteps: Timely 'State of Exception' Presents 'Human Cost' of Undocumented Workers Entering U.S. from Mexico; Exhibit at Institute of Humanities," Montage, University of Michigan, January 2013; www.montage.umich.edu/2013/01/follow-

ing-the-footsteps.

24. Suzanne Hesh, interviewed by author, April 14, 2015.

25. Ibid.

26. Daniela Pastrana, "A Memorial of White Scarves Protests Calderón's Legacy," Inter Press Service News Agency, www.ipsnews.net/2012/11/a-memorial-of-white-scarves-protests-calderons-legacy.

27. Suzanne Hesh interview.

28. Jody Ipsen interview.

29. Shura Wallin, interviewed by author, May 5, 2015.

30. Jody Ipsen interview.

31. Ibid.

32. Margaret Regan, "Fabric of Our Lives: Quilts with Powerful Messages are on Display at Tucson Meet Yourself," *Tucson Weekly*, Oct. 11, 2012. See the Red Cross Quilt in Helen Young Frost and Pam Knight Stevenson, *Grand Endeavors: Vintage Arizona Quilts and Their Makers* (Flagstaff, AZ: Northland Publishing, 1991), 79–81.

33. Laraine Daly Jones, email correspondence, May 7, 2015.

34. Jennifer Eschedor, interviewed by author, April 10, 2015.

35. Ibid.

36. Ibid.

37. "Quilters' Experiences," Los Desconocidos, losdesconocidos.org/quilter-experiences.

38. A similar embroidered Mexican textile, dated 1980s, is in the collection of The British Museum, AM1990.08.347.

39. "Los Desconocidos," Jennifer Eschedor: Artist and Teacher, eschasketch.com/my-art/los-desconocidos.

40. Jennifer Eschedor interview.

41. Jonathan Gregory, "Wrapped in Meanings: Quilts for Families of Soldiers Killed in the Afghanistan and Iraq Wars," in *Uncoverings* 31, ed. Laurel Horton (Lincoln, NE: American Quilt Study Group, 2010), 161–204.

42. Carolyn H. Krone and Thomas M. Horner, "Her Grief in the Quilt," in *Uncoverings* 13, ed. Laurel Horton (San Francisco, CA: American Quilt Study Group, 1992), 109–126.

43. Lawrence Howe, "A Text of the Times," 21.

44. Suzanne Hesh interview.

45. Cornelia Bayley, interviewed by the author, April 16, 2015.

46. Ibid.

47. Ibid.

48. Milagro means "miracle" in Spanish. The tiny metal religious forms used in Mexico and Latin America depict the object for which someone needs a miracle, such as a crippled leg, diseased heart or kidney, or a new house. They may represent a prayer or are offered in thanksgiving for prayers answered, and might be pinned to clothing on saint statues or hung on shrines. Eileen Oktavec, *Answered Prayers: Miracles and Milagros Along the Border* (Tucson: University of Arizona Press, 1995).

49. "Quilters' Experiences," *Los Desconocidos*.

50. Cornelia Bayley interview.

51. For more on Operation Streamline, see www.tucsonsamaritans.org/operation-streamline.html.

52. Nancy Amann, email correspondence, May 5, 2015.

53. Margaret Regan, *The Death of Josseline: Immigration Stories from the Arizona Border-lands* (Boston: Beacon Press, 2010), xix-xviii.

54. Nancy Amann email.

55. "Quilters' Experiences," *Los Desconocidos.*

56. Virgen de los Caminos, Smithsonian American Art Museum, 1996.77.

57. Laramie Treviño, "Stories in Stitches Tell of Peril, Hope/'Threads of Life' Sewing Project Also Helps Build Literacy in Southern Mendocino County," *SF Gate* (San Francisco), *Special to the Chronicle,* December 21, 2005.

58. "Death Lives in the Desert by Luz Maria 'Luzma' Bucio," Hilos de la Vida, *Art and Remembrance,* artandremembrance.org/hilos-de-la-vida-english/#mg_ld_1478.

59. Molly Johnson Martinez and Anderson Valley Artists, *Los Hilos de la Vida, Threads of Life: A Collection of Quilts & Stories* (publisher unknown, 2009); Karen Musgrave, "Los Hilos de la Vida (The Threads of Life)," *Quilters Newsletter,* December 2007, 36–39; Karen Musgrave, "Latina Quilts: Mexican Heritage and American Quiltmaking," in *Quilts Around the World: The Story of Quilting from Alabama to Zimbabwe,* ed. Spike Gillespie (Minneapolis, MN: Voyageur Press, 2010), 74–78.

60. Q.S.O.S. Interviews By Project: Los hilos de la vida QSOS, Quilt Alliance, www.allianceforamericanquilts.org.

61. April Shipp, *Strange Fruit: A Century of Lynching,* 2003, machine-pieced silk, cotton and corduroy, embroidered with cotton and metallic thread, 126 in. x 120 in., Michigan State University Museum, 08.

62. Kathleen Thompson and Hilary MacAustin, *The Face of Our Past: Images of Black Women from Colonial America to the Present* (Bloomington, IN: University of Indiana Press, 1999), 112.

63. April Shipp, www.quiltindex.org, record 1E-3D-225B.

64. Arlesa J. Shephard, "Quilts for McKinley: Women's Involvement in Politics," in *Uncoverings* 29, ed. Laurel Horton (Lincoln, NE: American Quilt Study Group, 2008), 138–157; and Jane Amelon, "The Persuasive Power of a Quilt: A Study of a Women's Prison Project," *Uncoverings* 30, ed. Laurel Horton (Lincoln, NE: American Quilt Study Group), 77–101.

65. Mary Worrall, Marsha MacDowell, and Lynne Swanson, *Quilts and Human Rights* (Lincoln, NE: University of Nebraska Press, 2016).

66. Mary Worrall, email correspondence, April 16, 2015.

67. Before I was invited to collaborate on a Migrant Quilt, I did not identify myself as an activist by any means. I was aware of the immigration crisis taking place just miles from my home, but it was not on my personal radar. Looking back, I am grateful that I received the opportunity to collaborate on a Migrant Quilt because it gave me a way to take a stand on an important issue. Cutting patches from denim jeans and inscribing them with the names of people I never knew was, first of all, an effort to dignify the memory of those who had died, but it also was an act of consciousness-raising unlike anything I had ever done.

68. Jody Ipsen interview.

69. Robin Reineke, email correspondence, May 19, 2015. Read more about her work at www.colibricenter.org/team.

70. Jody Ipsen interview.

Memorials of Satin: Funeral Ribbon Quilts in Context

Diana Bell-Kite

Gathering satin acetate florist ribbons from the gravesides of deceased loved ones and stitching them into quilts was widespread among working-class Southerners—black and white—from the mid-1940s through the early 1970s. Scholars have noted this unique form of commemorative quilting in passing, but have yet to examine the tradition's regionalism, its limited lifespan, and its relationship to wider trends in mid-twentieth century American society. Analyzing twenty-eight such quilts from eight states, along with professional florist literature, public documents, and oral interviews, exposes a distinctive regional culture in the midst of rapid transformation. This contextual study of funeral ribbon quilting reveals how changing memorial practices, growing consumerism, deep-seated frugality, and rapid technological innovation con-verged in the twentieth-century South.

Introduction

On a cool December day in 1955, Iona McNeill Thomas and her daughter, Lenora, visited the Broadway, North Carolina, cemetery where their late husband and father had been recently interred. Arriving at the plot, the women busied themselves with the task at hand: removing the colorful satin-acetate ribbons from the wilting flower arrangements that decorated his grave.[1] Claude Thomas had died in his sleep in the early hours of December 4.[2] Heart disease had plagued the aging farmer for years, and his death, while deeply saddening to those who loved him, had not been en-tirely unexpected. Recounting the day he died, granddaughter Janice Long said, "We were all awakened on that morning by my grandmother saying he had passed away." The family quickly alerted Charlie Rogers, a local fu-neral director, who embalmed the body and dressed it for that evening's wake at the Thomas home. Friends and neighbors brought food and flowers; they sat up through the night with Claude's body and kept his family company. The next morning, on December 5, the mourners, the body, and the flowers traveled to Mount Pisgah Presbyterian Church for Thomas's funeral. A graveside service followed, and finally, workers lowered the casket into the ground, filled in the grave, and arranged floral sprays over the freshly turned earth.

Janice Long later remembered that her mother and grandmother "waited about a week until the flowers didn't look good anymore" before removing the ribbons from the arrangements. The bows detached easily; they could "just take them off the flowers. They was [sic] pinned on there with this floral stick . . . all you had to do was just pull them off and then untie them." With ribbons in hand, the women returned home. In the following weeks and months, Iona Thomas carefully pressed the strips of synthetic fabric to remove wrinkles caused by bow knots and florist wire. She machine-pieced them together, adding batting, backing, and binding. Zigzag stitching along the seams held the three layers together. She thus turned the odd assortment of crumpled florist bows into a quilt (fig. 1). The jewel-toned creation contained thirty-two ribbons arranged in a strip pattern. It stretched over seven feet in length and more than six in width. Hues of bronze, yellow, gold, orange, red, pink, white, and purple gleamed in the sunlight.[3] Thomas folded the quilt carefully and packed it away.

Iona Thomas's actions in the aftermath of her husband's death were not unique. Rather, gathering funeral ribbons from the graves of deceased loved ones and stitching them into quilts was widespread among ordinary Southerners—black and white—from the mid-1940s through the early 1970s.[4] Quilt scholars have acknowledged the existence of funeral ribbon quilts in passing, but few have approached the subject in a comprehensive manner. In the only published article-length study of funeral ribbon quilting, "Symbols from Ribbons: Afro-American Funeral-Ribbon Quilts in Chatham County, North Carolina," Mary Anne McDonald considers the work of three quiltmakers: Laura Lee, Jennie Burnett, and Bessie Lee, who used funeral ribbons in their work. McDonald, writing in 1990, begins with the faulty assertion that "funeral ribbons are used exclusively by Afro-Americans" and limits her study to the quilts' symbolic functions and the "wider Afro-American attitudes toward death and burial" they reveal.[5] She equates the quilts' vivid chromatics and "improvisational sense of design" as "representative of the Afro-American quilt-making tradition."[6] Though McDonald notes that each of her three subjects "claimed

Fig. 1. Iona McNeill Thomas, Strip Quilt, Broadway, North Carolina, 1956. Satin acetate florist ribbon, pieced. 89 x 76 ½ inches. Made in memory of Claude Thomas. Courtesy of Janice Long. Photograph by Eric Blevins and D. Kent Thompson.

independent invention for the idea of using funeral ribbons in a quilt," she does not venture further to investigate the tradition's roots. Lynne Marrs Hammer Ferguson, in her unpublished paper, "Where Have All the Flowers Gone: A Study of a Funeral Ribbon Quilt," refutes McDonald's claim that only African Americans used funeral ribbons in quiltmaking as "clearly erroneous."[7] She examines two quilts that her great-grandmother, Roxie Belle Hall Hale of Tompkinsville, Kentucky, made from her great-grandfather's funeral ribbons and concludes that Hale's decision to use the material in quiltmaking was "likely a spontaneous creative endeavor."[8] Though Ferguson's study expands the scholarship on funeral ribbon quilting to include European-American makers, her focus on one quilter limits her capacity to identify and explain wider influences and trends.[9]

Other historians have noted the existence of funeral ribbon quilting briefly within broader studies. Gail Trechsel examines mourning quilts in the United States and focuses on the ways that quilts associated with death "provided the maker with a tangible memorial to the departed."[10] She interviewed a white Alabama quiltmaker, Bessie Alexander, who made strip quilts from her mother-in-law's funeral ribbons. Alexander "was not aware of other quilts of this type" but felt the need to make use of the abundance of ribbons she had carefully saved.[11] Trechsel concludes that "ribbon quilts are related to other mourning quilts in memorializing the dead and in the comfort they provide the maker." They allowed grieving women to create "a whole from fragments," which "serves an important psychological function to those in mourning."[12] Joyce Jones Newman, writing about North Carolina quilting, notes in passing that one "type of memory quilt made in several areas was constructed of ribbons from the bows of floral wreaths sent to the funeral of a family member or friend."[13] Cuesta Benberry identifies a spread made of pieced funeral ribbons in her study of black Arkansan quilters. She suggests that the Central Medallion piece may be a coffin cover, rather than a quilt top, remarking that "in rural black communities while homemade coffin covers are not plentiful household items, they are not uncommon."[14] Though she presents an intriguing subject, Benberry offers little documentation to guide future study. These scholars' investigations of the symbolic and memorial functions of funeral ribbon quilts deliver some clues as to the quilts' origins and meanings. However, they stop short of providing a broader context for the tradition's regionalism, limited lifespan, and its relationship to wider developments within twentieth-century American consumerism and commemorative practices.

A study of twenty-eight funeral ribbon quilts from eight states reveals the existence of a vibrant regional tradition in the South and raises questions about broader trends in mid-twentieth century American society.[15] The quilts identified in this study were made within a period of thirty-eight years. Annie Phillips Vaughan of Elba, Alabama, created the earliest in 1946, and Blanche Hux, of Twin City, Georgia, made the latest in 1984.[16] While women have memorialized their loved ones through quilting for centuries, the use of funeral ribbons in such quilts appears to have been limited to a distinct historical period.[17] An examination of changing American memorial practices preceding and comprising this time frame helps contextualize the tradition.

Before the Civil War, Americans overwhelmingly tended to the dead within their own homes and families. Death was a frequent visitor. High mortality rates due to infectious disease, childbirth, accidents, and limited access to effective healthcare meant that eighteenth- and early-nineteenth-century Americans knew death much more intimately than their contemporary counterparts. When a family member died, relatives bathed and dressed the corpse, laid it out, built the coffin, dug the grave, and placed the remains in it. The Civil War changed this relationship between the living and the dead dramatically. Hundreds of thousands of young men died and were buried far from home, and families could no longer care for their loved ones in customary ways.[18]

While various corpse-preservation technologies have existed for millennia, arterial embalming came into its own and gained widespread acceptance during the Civil War. Those who could afford to have their deceased sons and husbands brought home from distant battlefields and military hospitals sought to have the remains preserved for transport. After the war, embalming continued to gain popularity, and a new class of morticians—many of whom had honed their skills embalming dead soldiers—started businesses and formed professional organizations with their peers. Not only did they embalm, these new "funeral directors," according to historian Gary Laderman, "became the primary managers of the corpse and the ceremonies to dispose of it."[19] From securing a casket to washing and dressing the body and communicating with clergy, funeral directors gradually assumed the duties families had traditionally managed. Urbanization, industrialization, the rise of hospitals, and an overall decrease in mortality supported this transition during the late nineteenth and early twentieth centuries. Families lived farther from extended kinship networks than they had in the past; death occurred more frequently in hospitals than at home; medical advances lessened the impact of infectious disease. People were relieved to let professionals handle the business of death. By the 1920s, funeral homes became, according to Laderman, "the primary location for carrying out the responsibilities associated with burial."[20]

This was not the case in the South. While antebellum Southern funerals did not vary significantly from those in other regions, historian Charles Reagan Wilson asserts, "In the late 19th and early 20th centuries, Southern funerals came to differ from those in the rest of the nation."[21] Postwar poverty beleaguered most Southerners, white and black. The overwhelmingly rural character of the region and the centrality of evangelical Protestantism caused people to persist "in old-fashioned ways" in memorial practice.[22] Most Southern families continued to tend to their own dead as their antebellum forebears had done, washing and dressing corpses, sitting up with them, and burying them quickly before the Southern climate took its toll on the unpreserved remains. While new funeral directors set up shop in Northern and Midwestern cities in the late 1800s, few Southern communities were large enough to support a funeral home. Few potential clients were prosperous enough to afford undertaking services, and many harbored doubts about the moral and religious propriety of altering the "sacred remains" through embalming.[23]

Slowly, the region did begin to adapt to the new national model. By the end of World War II, Southerners had largely embraced the funeral director's central role in caring for the dead and the utility of embalming.[24] However, as Wilson notes, "even when the American funeral industry conquered the South, it took on sectional dimensions."[25] Practices like sitting up with corpses (still in private homes in many instances), open casket funerals, evangelical sermons, and expressive grief at services still differentiated Southern funerals from their counterparts in the North and Midwest.[26] As a holdover from earlier times when embalming was unavailable or undesirable, Southerners continued to bury bodies sooner after death than typical in other regions.[27] Additionally, the immense waves of turn-of-the century immigration that had infused many parts of the country with a vast diversity of death practices and traditions left the South virtually untouched. Though the funeral industry had become entrenched by the 1940s, funerals in the South remained markedly Southern.

With the rise of funeral directors and funeral homes nationwide, a group of allied businesses also professionalized and prospered. Casket manufacturers, chemical producers, automobile companies, and cosmetics firms rode the wave of commercialization.[28] So did florists. Whereas antebellum Americans may have gathered or arranged their own flowers when possible to spread on a fresh grave, professionally crafted floral designs gained popularity as the new funeral industry flourished. Wreaths and standing sprays featuring mourning phrases and donor names surrounded corpses during viewings and decorated graves.[29] Florist organizations worked to instill in consumers the sense that sending flowers to funerals was more than just a kind gesture—it was a moral obligation. One writer couched this sentiment in terms of religious duty: "Floral expressions of sympathy are not just a meaningless social custom among Christians. Rather they are symbolic of a genuine sharing of sorrow and grief, an exchange between friends and the deceased's surviving family of those firm hopes, unshakable joys, and ageless convictions which constitute the confidence of the Christian living and dead."[30] The marketing worked, and by the mid-twentieth century, "65 to 70 percent of the entire flower industry sales [were] for sympathy flowers."[31]

Like all florists, Southerners depended on the availability of a variety of fresh flowers from nearby and distant growers to be able to supply their customers. The South's rural character and lesser-developed infrastructure compared with other parts of the country kept florists in a state of near-constant anxiety about supply. While flowers grew well in the region, florists were limited to seasonal blooms. Ione Garrett Colquette, an Alabama florist who went into business with her father before World War II, remembered that in the early days "we had sweet-peas. We could use them for just about everything. . . . We'd get blue bells and cape jasmine from Texas. Those were our two mainstays in the spring." In summer "there were geraniums that we used for funeral sprays and there were gladiolus. That was about all of the cut flower crop."[32] Florists could order stock from afar, but the turnaround time was slow. Colquette explained, "A lot of wild smilax was used. It came from the Carolinas and it took three to four weeks to get it."[33]

Unsurprisingly, weekly regional and national professional florist journals reported closely on flower availability at important markets. *Florists' Review's* Atlanta correspondent informed readers during the first week of April 1954 that "roses were again on the short side with just enough supply to fill the regular orders." Likewise, "carnations were fair. Although supply was limited."[34] Journals also offered tips for making the most out of existing inventory. In a report from a North Carolina florist association meeting, one expert counseled members how to "revive stock" by "dunk[ing] flower heads in cold water for an hour or less, then mash[ing] the stems and remove[ing] most of the foliage."[35] Ione Colquette remembered an ice box used to preserve flowers: "It held a 300-pound block of ice. If it wasn't for that ice box, we wouldn't have kept fresh roses."[36]

While florists could plan ahead for weddings or the Easter rush, they had very little notice for funerals and often had to scramble to keep enough fresh blooms on hand. With supply and quality unreliable, the death of a particularly prominent individual could easily wipe out a florist's entire flower stock. Some, when faced with more demand than inventory, scraped the bottom of the proverbial barrel in order to provide flowers. Floral design expert Georgia Effertz noted that "too many florists have been guilty of sending wilted, old blooms in funeral pieces."[37] Others compensated for the lack of flowers with ribbon. Longtime Randolph County, North Carolina, florist Michael Trogdon remembered his predecessors commenting that when flowers were scarce, they would "use more ribbon to make a nicer presentation for customers. [The ribbon] was a more integral part of the wreath than it is today."[38] (fig. 2) This practice also brought criticism from Effertz: "Some florists think they can mask wilted flowers by smothering them with large amounts of ribbon—cheap ribbon. Nothing detracts more from the rich beauty of flowers than great amounts of sleazy ribbon."[39]

This overcompensation with ribbon became possible due to the development of abundant, affordable, synthetic satin in the mid-twentieth-century. The Celanese Corporation first produced cellulose acetate commercially in the United States in 1924.[40] Prior to World War II, however, the material proved cost-prohibitive for most floral designs. Ione Colquette remembered, "Satin came along as ribbon material but it was expensive at first. It was used for weddings mostly."[41] Rather, florists often

Fig. 2. This standing wreath (left), prepared by Raleigh, NC, florist Woody Roberson, illustrates the centrality of ribbon in mid-twentieth-century southern funeral designs. Note how Roberson used ribbon both in the large central bow and to wrap the circular form. *Southern Florist & Nurseryman* 86, no. 12 (June 29, 1973): 40.

designed with maline, an open mesh similar to tulle.[42] Satin acetate gradually became inexpensive and plentiful, and by the late 1940s it was ubiquitous.[43] The material had a lustrous sheen, could be dyed brilliant colors, and closely resembled silk. Florists found it to be the perfect accompaniment to flower arrangements, and this research suggests that Southerners in particular used it in great volumes.

Regional funeral traditions shaped the way Southerners bought flowers and the way florists designed them. Anthropologist Christopher Crocker found that floral arrangements played an important role in Southern funerals in the mid-twentieth century. "There was no particular symbolic importance in the variety of flowers used. Rather, it [was] form, size, and quantity of the 'floral tributes' which [were] emphasized."[44] Different arrangements had different meanings. Family members and those closest to the deceased tended to bestow standing wreaths and casket sprays. "The contribution of such displays" according to Crocker, "be[came] a social declaration of the closeness of relationship to the deceased and, consequently, of the importance of the loss suffered."[45] For those who had "suffered a loss but who are not regarded as 'bereaved,'" the standing spray tended to be the arrangement of choice. Standing sprays featured a one-sided floral design that was flat on the back and supported by a wire easel (fig. 3). Georgia Effertz labeled them "old fashioned," but conceded that "in some parts of the country, the spray . . . outsells the arrangement two-to-one."[46] Such was the case in the South, where savvy consumers favored the design because "it gave the customer a good showing for his money."[47] With size and quantity of arrangements carrying ample social weight, the economical yet splashy spray made a big impression.

The relatively quick turnaround time between wake/visitation and burial in many Southern services afforded florists leeway that other regional traditions did not. For much of the twentieth century, florists designed wreaths and sprays on straw, moss, or foam forms.[48] While such arrangements proved relatively lightweight and portable, the forms lacked a water source, and flowers could not survive lengthy display. According to Michael Trogdon, "You'd be crossing your fingers that the flowers would hold up for both the visitation and the funeral because there was no water source." These types of designs proved impractical in areas of the country where multiple days of visitation preceded a funeral service or where mourners expected to appreciate floral offerings for an extended time period. Basket arrangements or other styles where stems could re-

Fig. 3. Standing sprays, like this example from the mid-1970s, tended to be the design of choice for southern funerals. *Southern Florist & Nurseryman* 88, no. 4 (April 18, 1975): 27.

main in water proved more realistic for multiday affairs.[49] For Southern funerals, however, sprays and wreaths were by far the arrangements of choice.

Florists' ribbon selection correlated closely with arrangement style. According to Trogdon, during the 1950s and 1960s in Randolph County, "#100-width [4-inch] satin ribbon was used 98% of the time on funeral designs" like sprays and wreaths. Lynn Sanders Wilkinson, a longtime florist from Durham, North Carolina, recalled, "Another ribbon that is used in the floral industry and has been used since 1950 is a #40 width satin ribbon (100% acetate) measuring 2 ½ inches."[50] These two widths were among the widest ribbon that florists employed, and they adorned the majority of Southern funeral work. Florist Patsy Hale of Tompkinsville, Kentucky, explained to researcher Lynne Marrs Hammer Ferguson that in the 1960s florists used about 2 1/3 yards of ribbon per bow.[51] They would also add on streamers of one-to-two feet in length that had been cut separately.[52] Likewise, design style and scale influenced the amount of ribbon used. Trogdon reflected, "If you were doing a round wreath, you would sometimes put two bows on that at the top and bottom—at 11:00 and 5:00 off center. You'd have longer pieces in bigger bows and sprays." For arrangements other than wreaths and sprays, thinner ribbons tended to be used, and bows did not play as central a role in the overall design. The #9 (1 5/16-inch) width often adorned potted plants, and in basket arrangements, "there may [have] be[en] a small bow on the handle," but the bow was certainly not the focal point.[53]

In many communities, "flower girls," selected from among the deceased person's female relatives or from a Sunday school class, would transport the arrangements from cars into the church for the funeral. Joyce Robinson Broyles of Roane County, Tennessee, remembered, "Back then people got so many flowers. Schoolgirls were like flower girls. They carried the flowers whenever somebody's relative died."[54] The girls would process down the aisle and position floral tributes around the casket until all those given had been carefully displayed for the mourners to see. Some also carried the flowers from the church to the graveside. This tradition persisted longer in black funerals than in white, but saw widespread practice in both communities. The custom emphasized the quantity and size of arrangements given and highlighted the flowers as a critically important part of the funeral service.[55]

Into this distinctive memorial culture, where funerals and the arrangements sent to them bore a markedly regional flavor, the practice of making quilts from funeral ribbons was born. In addition to the date range and region in which they were made, the quilts considered in this study shared numerous other similarities. The women who made them tended not to hail from elite society but rather from the rural working-class majority. Most had only an elementary education, though approximately a quarter had completed some high school. One, who taught school in rural Alabama, had gone to college for two years.[56] Several of the quiltmakers lived on family farms. Two worked in textile mills, and those who worked within the home were married to coal miners, fishermen, truck drivers, and day laborers.[57] Women from these backgrounds were accustomed to quilting from recycled fabrics, and they were likely more willing than their upper-class counterparts to expend the time and effort necessary to collect, process, and piece together florist ribbons.

Quiltmakers' descendants and relatives overwhelmingly attributed the desire to make ribbon quilts to a deeply ingrained sense of frugality. Mary Clement Allen, whose grandmother Susie Ferguson Noland McKnight made a quilt in 1964 in Crabtree, North Carolina, from her late sister's ribbons, remembered, "They didn't waste anything. Satin was not something they had in abundance."[58] Likewise, Sibbie Veal Warrick of Elba, Alabama, remembered that her aunt Annie Phillips Vaughan, who made quilts in memory of her mother and niece, "could use everything for something."[59] Ruth Moose's mother, Vera Smith Morris, made a quilt in 1971 in Albemarle, North Carolina, from her deceased husband's bows. Moose believed "the tradition is not to waste anything, to use it up, make something memorable, a keepsake of sorts."[60]

This near compulsion to exercise thrift in all aspects of life was not the only factor that inspired women to make funeral ribbon quilts. Some adopted the practice after seeing other such bedcovers. Vera Smith Morris "saw one someone else had made" and had the idea that a quilt could be made from her husband's funeral ribbons as well.[61] Likewise, for Susie Ferguson Noland McKnight, "someone else they knew had made one and they got the idea from her."[62] As with all styles and fashions, peer-to-peer transmission tended to be an effective means of dissemination.

The ages of the makers ranged from the youngest at forty to the eldest at seventy-five. The average age was sixty-two.[63] At this stage of life they were beyond their hectic childbearing years and likely had more time for creative endeavors. Further, they were at an age where husbands, siblings, and other loved ones had begun passing on; yet they were not so elderly as to be unable to quilt. Finally, these women came from a generation and social class that had learned to quilt out of necessity. They had made bed-coverings from feed sacks and old work clothes; their family members slept under multiple homemade quilts to stay warm on winter nights.[64] Their work had little to do with the quilting revival of the 1970s—rather they used newly available materials in a craft tradition they had practiced throughout their lives.[65]

Of the sample studied, white women made twenty of the quilts, black women made five, and the makers' racial identity was unknown for three pieces.[66] While hardly an exhaustive investigation, the data clearly calls into question any claim that only African-Americans or only European-Americans made funeral ribbon quilts. Though some funereal traditions tended to be associated more closely with one community or the other, fu-neral ribbon quilting crossed the boundaries of segregated society. Fur-ther, the qualities that Mary Anne McDonald claimed as indicative of African American quilting—the use of bold color and improvisational de-sign—apply to nearly all of the quilts considered. Recycled ribbons were thin, brightly colored, slippery, and challenging to sew: practically the per-fect formula for such a quilt. Moreover, black women made one of the most symmetrical, least improvisational quilts in the sample, supporting recent scholarship critiquing the notion that a maker's cultural back-ground can be discerned solely from viewing her work.[67]

Not only did the quiltmakers share many similarities, so did their de-ceased loved ones. The individuals memorialized by ribbon quilts were both male and female and tended to die of natural causes in their senior years. Excepting one quilt made for an infant, the average age of the dece-dents was sixty-nine. Where a cause of death was known (which was only the case for about a third of the quilts studied), documents revealed that five succumbed to heart disease, two to cancer, one to a gastrointestinal hemorrhage, and one to a pulmonary embolism.[68] None of the quilts studied memorialized accident or murder victims, individuals who died tragically young (other than the aforementioned infant), or people who perished due to other "unnatural" causes. Further, while the majority of the decedents were aged, they were not ancient. They still had large-enough living peer and family networks to receive ample floral offerings at their funerals. The quilts in this sample seem to have been made in cele-bration of reasonably long lives well lived rather than in memory of those cut dramatically short.

Most of the makers followed similar processes in turning florist bows

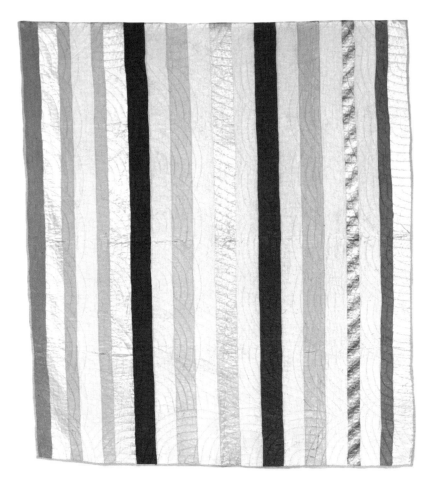

Fig. 4. Sadie Mae Hawks Cook, Strip Quilt, Beckley, West Virginia, c. 1958. Satin acetate florist ribbon, pieced. 79 1/2 x 65 1/2 inches. Made in memory of Edward Hamilton Cook. West Virginia Heritage Quilt Project Collection, West Virginia State Archives.

into quilts. Mary Clement Allen remembered that women in her family would "go get [the ribbons] from the grave before it rained." Satin acetate did not hold up well after becoming wet. Michael Trogdon explained, "Acetate says it's weather-resistant and it repels a little bit of water but after much rain it wilts."[69] To preserve the fabric for optimal use, timely collection proved important. After removing the bows from arrangements, women would untie them and remove any florist wire. The ribbons would then inevitably require pressing to remove wrinkles and creases. Ruth Moose "knew [her mother] ironed all the ribbons before she made the quilt." Sherlie Walker, granddaughter of Roxie Belle Hall Hale, who made a quilt from her husband's ribbons, remembered that her grandmother "took the ribbons and pressed them flat."[70] If makers did not intend to begin sewing immediately, they had to store the ribbons carefully to prevent re-creasing. Susie Ferguson Noland McKnight "saved up ribbons on a coat hanger and kept them flat until she started sewing on them."[71] Annie Phillips Vaughan rolled ribbons to keep them from wrinkling.[72]

All of the quilts studied in this sample were pieced, and the makers overwhelmingly used sewing machines to accomplish this part of the process. Most pieced the ribbons side-to-side in a strip pattern. This approach required the least amount of labor and to a certain extent preserved the original shapes and sizes of the ribbons. Sadie Mae Hawks Cook, of Beckley, West Virginia, made a strip quilt from her father-in-law, Edward Hamilton Cook's, ribbons. His floral arrangements clearly included bows made of both #100 and #40 ribbons as the width differences are evident in the finished quilt (fig. 4). She seemed to have only included bows in the quilt, as the twenty unbroken lengths of ribbon all stretched 79 ½ inches.[73] Others included both bow ribbon and streamers in their creations. An unknown maker, who used ribbons from Margaret Irene Wicker's Sanford, North Carolina, grave in 1958, pieced two quilts. While one incorporates mostly whole ribbons, the other also showcases multiple streamers hemmed end to end and side to side (fig. 5).[74] Though most strip quilters pieced their ribbons perpendicularly, one unknown maker, likely from Alabama, situated her strips diagonally, giving the quilt a dynamic sense of motion (fig. 6).[75]

Some quilters tackled more complex patterns. Annie Phillips Vaughan made two Center Medallion quilts that roughly resembled an Around the World quilt or a single Log Cabin block (figs. 7, 8, 9).[76] Pearl Harris Evans of Macon, North Carolina, pieced ribbons from her brother-in-law's funeral arrangements into an eighty-eight-block lattice pattern design (fig. 10).[77] A group of black fishermen's wives from Cedar Island, North Carolina, made an elaborate Diamond Star quilt from the ribbons taken off of Sylvester Ross Goodwin's grave. A North Carolinian by birth who had relocated to Pennsylvania to open a seafood business, Goodwin maintained personal and professional ties with the fishermen and their wives throughout his life. After his death, his wife, Bertha, collected his

Fig. 5. Maker unknown, Strip Quilt, Sanford, North Carolina, 1958. Satin acetate florist ribbon, pieced. 87 1/4 x 82 inches. Made in memory of Margaret Irene Wicker. Collection of the North Carolina Museum of History, Raleigh, NC, 1993.221.1. Photograph by Eric Blevins and D. Kent Thompson.

ribbons and mailed them to the North Carolina women. They turned the raw ribbons into a quilt and mailed it back to Bertha in memory of her husband.[78]

One of the most characteristic qualities of funeral ribbon quilts is their vibrant coloration. Though makers generally had little choice in the colors available for use—florists and their clients determined this well in advance of any quiltmaking activity—most quilters distinguished their creations in the ways they chose to juxtapose and display the ribbons. Bessie Alexander of Cordova, Alabama, "organized the colors symmetrically, beginning with deep lavender at the center of the quilt. The other colors—red, yellow, orange, and olive—fan[ned] out, in pairs, on either

Fig. 6. Maker unknown, Strip Quilt, possibly Alabama, ca. 1945–1975. Satin acetate florist ribbon, pieced. 85 x 62 inches. Photo courtesy of the National Museum of Funeral History, Houston, Texas.

Fig. 7. Annie Phillips Vaughan, Central Medallion Quilt, Elba, Alabama, 1946. Satin acetate florist ribbon, pieced. 56 x 62 1/2 inches. Made in memory of Mary Jane Phillips Veal. North Carolina Quilt Project, courtesy of the North Carolina Museum of History.

side of the first lavender ribbon."[79] An unknown Arkansan used red ribbon to create a center square and borders. She then filled in the body of the spread with alternating pink, yellow, and white ribbon to create symmetry (fig. 11).[80] Iona Thomas staggered the light and dark ribbons to better highlight the different colors in her quilt. Rather than putting all of the reds or bronzes together, she intermingled them with white and light pink to create visual interest (fig. 1).[81] According to Ruth Moose, Vera Smith Morris's quilt "was lovely since she blended the colors nicely."

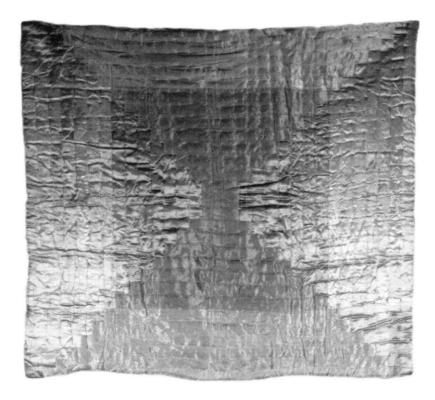

Fig. 8. Annie Phillips Vaughan, Central Medallion Quilt, Elba, Alabama, 1954. Satin acetate florist ribbon, pieced. 59 x 67 inches. Made in memory of Debbie Gail Warrick. North Carolina Quilt Project, courtesy of the North Carolina Museum of History.

Though makers had little control over the colors available for quilting, ribbon colors were far from randomly chosen. Many factors determined how florists selected the hues they used. The colors and types of flowers chosen for arrangements drove the ribbon selection. In some arrangements, florists intended for ribbon color to harmonize with the flowers. Patsy Hale explained to Lynn Marrs Hammer Ferguson that dark red ribbon often accented red roses and gold could accompany mums. Printed ribbons sometimes helped blend an arrangement. Red and white striped ribbon, for example, harmonized with red and white carnations.[82] According to Michael Trogdon, blue "could have been used for asters which can be lavender/blue and gladiolas." As a contrasting color, green ribbon was sometimes used on arrangements with white flowers.[83] Season

Fig. 9. Reverse of Vaughan quilt, 1954. North Carolina Quilt Project, courtesy of the North Carolina Museum of History.

and flower availability also influenced ribbon choice. If a florist had only a few varieties in stock, likely only ribbons that matched those flowers would be used.

The deceased person's gender played an important role in flower and ribbon selection. After seeing one of the quilts made in memory of Margaret Irene Wicker, Michael Trogdon commented, "I knew it was from a woman's funeral. I could tell because it had so much pink, lavender, yellow, and red." His predecessors, the Burges, "were very particular about gender colors. They would not have sent pink flowers to a man's funeral unless it was specifically requested by the client." Likewise, orange and bronze tended to be reserved for men. White, yellow, and lavender were used for both sexes, as was red, though red appeared more frequently in men's arrangements.[84] When Sibbie Veal Warrick's infant daughter died in

1954, her aunt, Annie Phillips Vaughan, made her a ribbon quilt as a memorial to her baby. Clearly florists took note of the decedent's age and gender as the quilt contains ample pale pink with some light yellow and pale gray (figs. 8, 9). Professional florist literature supported clear gender differentiation in funeral designs. Writing for *Florists' Review*, Doris Ann Krupinski asserted that "there is at least one aspect of the deceased that the florist can act upon: His gender."[85] She urged florists to use gender-appropriate colors, warning that if they failed to do so, bereaved family "members would subconsciously realize that there was something wrong with the picture."

The quilting styles makers used to join top, backing, and batting varied widely and, to a certain extent, revealed their differing intentions for their creations. Annie Phillips Vaughan thickly batted both of her quilts and tied them rather than stitching the layers together. She was also the only quiltmaker in the study who pieced both the top and the backing of her bedcoverings entirely of florist ribbons (fig. 9).[86] Her quilting style indicates that she expected her spreads to be used for warmth. Additionally, she could have made a larger quilt or multiple quilts without piecing the backing had her intention been solely to display the ribbons. A few makers hand-quilted their bedcoverings. The North Carolina fishermen's wives quilted Sylvester Goodwin's ribbons with a chevron pattern that complemented the Diamond Star quilt top.[87] Sadie Mae Hawks Cook quilted in the free-form fan pattern ubiquitous in Southern utility quilts.[88] Others made use of their sewing machines. The machine-quilted pieces tended to be thinly batted if batted at all—likely due in part to the struggle that home machines of the 1950s and 1960s would have endured to stitch through thick layers. Also, as evidenced by another technique that machine quilters used widely, they probably intended for the quilts to serve a decorative rather than utilitarian purpose. Domestic sewing machines with a zigzag option had arrived in the United States in the late 1940s, and funeral ribbon quilters made extensive use of the stitch.[89] Several strip quilts from North Carolina featured machine zigzag quilting stitches that followed the lengthwise piecing seams in colors contrasting to the ribbons (fig. 12).[90] Not only did the stitches help the seams lay flat, they added a decorative element similar to the herringbone and feather stitches so frequently seen on crazy quilts from the late nineteenth and early twentieth centuries. Pearl Harris Evans, another Tar Heel, did not add batting or backing to her lattice-pattern quilt top, but she did hand embroider a zigzag pattern over the bedcovering's seams.[91] Whether this was a local-

Fig. 10. Pearl Harris Evans, Lattice Quilt, Macon, North Carolina, c. 1951–1958. Satin acetate florist ribbon, pieced. 63 x 86 inches. Made in memory of Willie Raymond Riggan, North Carolina Quilt Project, courtesy of the North Carolina Museum of History.

Fig. 11. Unknown maker, Central Medallion Quilt Top, Cotton Plant, Arkansas, c. 1970. Satin acetate florist ribbon, pieced. 76 1/2 x 69 inches. Collection of the Old State House Museum, Little Rock, AR, 1995.014.01.

ized variation intended to convey the quilts' ornamental purpose or rather a coincidence among the quilts sampled is unclear. A few quilts with attached backing featured no quilting or batting whatsoever—a clue that these makers prioritized decorative function in their designs.[92]

Certainly, funeral ribbon quilts' meanings varied by maker.[93] For many, this particular style of quilting permitted reflection on the sympathy expressed for their families during a difficult time. According to Christopher Crocker, in the mid-twentieth-century South, "there [was] a general correlation drawn between the number, size, and approximate cost of the flowers and the deceased's social position."[94] For bereaved families who received enough arrangements to make an entire quilt from the ribbons, this community outpouring certainly conveyed a great deal of respect and esteem for the deceased. Ruth Moose remembered her mother

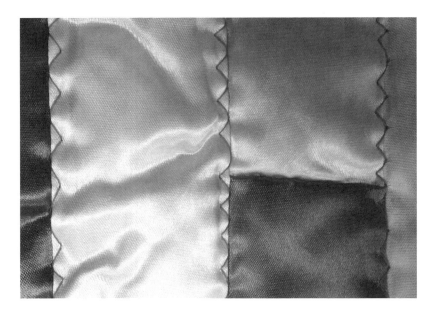

Fig. 12. Maker unknown, Strip Quilt detail, Sanford, North Carolina, 1958. Satin acetate florist ribbon, pieced. 87 ¼ x 82 inches. Made in memory of Margaret Irene Wicker. Many North Carolina makers quilted their creations using a machine zigzag stitch. Collection of the North Carolina Museum of History, Raleigh, NC, 1993.221.1.

"being proud there were so many ribbons, enough to make a lap quilt." Michael Trogdon also drew connections between the number of arrangements sent and families' gratification: "People look at the flowers and think 'this many people cared about [the deceased].' People look at it with pride and are warmed by it and comforted by it." The size of the funeral ribbon quilt communicated this concept—the larger the quilt, the greater the perceived care and concern the family received during their grief. The dimensions of the quilts in this sample varied considerably since the makers had vastly differing numbers of ribbons with which to sew. Some, like Vera Morris, had enough ribbons to create a lap quilt. Others, such as Bessie Alexander, who made four quilts from her mother-in-law's ribbons, had more.[95]

Few quilt owners were able to articulate how ribbon quilt makers—all now deceased—had felt about their completed quilts. However, the myriad ways the makers used their completed creations does offer some clues. Satin acetate ribbon proved far less sturdy than most materials used for quilting in the mid-twentieth century.[96] Further, the emotional impact the ribbons carried brought an additional layer of preciousness. Some permitted hands-off viewing. Roxie Hale displayed her quilts "in 1965 and possibly in 1966. They were then stored away in a dresser drawer in [her] guest room."[97] Maddie Elizabeth Evans Robinson of Midtown, Tennessee, who made a quilt from her husband's ribbons, "had a room that nobody ever slept in. She put it on that bed. Nobody ever went in that room. She wouldn't let anybody touch it."[98] Bertha Stickler Goodwin's quilt "was put in a cedar chest and never displayed."[99] Similarly, Mary Cox Trogdon of Ramseur, North Carolina, "never used [her quilt] on any bed."[100] Others actually used their ribbon quilts. After viewing one of Laura Lee's quilts, Mary Anne McDonald noted that it had "obviously been used, not stored away in a chest."[101] Susie Ferguson Noland McKnight kept her ribbon quilt on her bed, as did Vera Morris.[102] Though Iona Thomas's quilt "was just packed away and you didn't even see it," her granddaughter Janice Long remembered, someone did use it eventually. Janice Long's daughter, Leslie Cox, remembered as a teenager she "loved the quilt. I thought it was just beautiful. And so I don't think I asked, I just went into [Long's] closet and took the quilt and used it—and spread it on my bed. So I must have thought I wasn't supposed to."[103] Clearly different makers and owners had varying levels of comfort with how their quilts should be treated and differing perceptions of the bedcoverings' significance.

For Ruth Moose, her father's funeral ribbons carried great emotional power. Before her mother, Vera Smith Morris, stitched them into a quilt, Morris actually suggested that Moose should be the one to make the bedcovering. Unable to bring herself to do so, Moose declined and instead expressed her feelings through another creative outlet—writing. In her short story "The Wreath-Ribbon Quilt," Moose depicts a bereaved daughter whose mother presents her with a bag of carefully pressed funeral ribbons. The ribbons cause the daughter to have flashbacks to her father's funeral: "In my mind I see the wreaths still, my Father's frozen face, the scar untouched; not even the undertakers would try to camouflage it," and she cannot agree to make the quilt. "'No,' I shake my head. 'No.'"[104] In her fictionalized account, Moose conveys the real-life depth of emotion that funeral ribbons and the quilts made from them could muster.

By the early 1970s, funeral ribbon quilting was on the decline. Several factors brought about this downturn. Since the funeral industry's emergence, vocal critics had called into question the ethics of those who made their living in the profession. According to Gary Laderman, "Public indictments of the American funeral, and disturbing questions about profiting from the death of others, haunted men and women involved in this enterprise throughout the century."[105] In 1963 the discourse reached a new level. British-born journalist Jessica Mitford published a scathing exposé of the American funeral profession, *The American Way of Death*, which accused funeral directors of unethical practices and widespread price gouging. They preyed, she asserted, upon unsuspecting grief-stricken families at the most vulnerable time of their lives.[106] Her book became a bestseller and, according to Laderman, "marked a turning point in American attitudes toward disposal of the dead." He concluded, "Funeral directing in particular would never be the same again."[107]

Florists did not escape Mitford's ire. "The undertaker," she wrote, "has generally drawn the spotlight upon himself when the high cost of dying has come under scrutiny. But he is not the whole show. Behind the scenes, waiting for their cue, are the cemeteries, florists, monument makers, vault manufacturers."[108] She criticized the "deluge" of flowers that accompanied funerals and the high cost of providing such an ephemeral product. The blooms were even impossible to give away since their forms so distinctly communicated their gloomy purpose.[109]

For their part, florist associations fought back against Mitford's critiques and against larger trends toward omitting funeral flowers altogether. Such "please omit" messages had been appearing in obituaries with increasing and alarming frequency in the 1960s, prompted by high-profile funerals where charitable donations had been suggested in lieu of flowers. Georgia Effertz called this tendency "phony nobility under the guise of 'helping the family,'" and a "flagrant discrimination of the floral industry."[110] The American Florists Marketing Council (AFMC) printed a leaflet for distribution by members titled "Sympathy Flowers—New Dimensions in Caring." The piece "opens with personal insight into one person's thoughts upon the death of a close friend. The reflection follows the mental process of deciding what to do to let the bereaved family know of one's grief, sympathy and wish to help."[111] Unsurprisingly, the grief-stricken friend decides to send sympathy flowers and realizes how the gesture "enables him to express his sentiment in a personal, individualized manner."[112] The AFMC also published full-page ads in *Reader's Digest* and other popular journals in order to disseminate its message to consumers.

Despite their best efforts, florists could not turn the tide of public opinion back toward sympathy flowers. Though Southerners, as usual, clung to old ways longer than those in other regions, Southern florists too

Fig. 13. New weatherproof florist ribbon, like this "Fibra-Satin" design came onto the market during the mid–1970s and largely replaced acetate. Southern Florist & Nurseryman 87, no. 30 (October 18, 1974): 38.

felt the pinch of "please omit." According to Michael Trogdon, "funeral business today is not a drop in the bucket compared to when I started in the late 1970s. It used to be standard to have a funeral with 50 floral designs. Everything [sic] you had a connection with would honor your life with flowers." Nowadays, "flowers are not sent as much as they once were." With declining emphasis on funeral flowers and specifically on their power to convey a deceased person's social standing, ribbon quilters lacked the material and the motivation to continue their craft.

Further, the generation of women who had embraced funeral ribbon quilting during its three decades of popularity was dying out. Their daughters and granddaughters, raised in a world of urbanization, consumerism, and vast societal change, largely lost touch with their foremothers' stitching skills and deeply ingrained frugality. Though the Bicentennial-era quilting revival prompted some to pick up their needles, creations pieced from laboriously collected and pressed funeral ribbons tended not to be at the forefront of new quilters' agendas.

Finally, and most tangibly impactful, florists overwhelmingly ceased using satin acetate ribbon in funeral designs during the mid-1970s. New polypropylene products like Fibra-Satin® and Flora-Satin® debuted and quickly pushed acetate out of the market. According to Michael Trogdon, "it first came into use in the seventies and it was first used in arrangements that go on graves because it's weatherproof" (fig. 13). Unlike acetate, which wilted soon after contact with water, polypropylene would hold up to the heaviest of deluges. Further, Trogdon remarked, "it costs less than acetate and the consumer can't tell the difference." One key distinction between the two materials was that polypropylene was "more plasticky—you can tear it. It would never sew because it would crack where you'd try to sew it." If that were not enough to render funeral ribbon quilting a lost art, most florists switched to thinner ribbon. Trogdon explained, many "stopped using #100 in the late 1970s because it's more expensive and more difficult to tie . . . many new people in the business don't know how to tie it." New technology, new lifestyles, and new trends in memorial culture thus collectively brought about the demise of the funeral ribbon quilt.[113]

After Iona McNeill Thomas finished making her ribbon quilt in 1956 and packed it away, she rarely spoke about it. However, her granddaughter, Janice Long, believed the quilt did hold significance for Thomas because "that was her husband's—[the ribbons] came off his grave." Long inherited the quilt after her mother's death and continues to cherish it for the memories it holds of both her late grandfather and of the woman who made it. She intends to "pass it down to one of [her] granddaughters" in the future. Funeral ribbon quilting, as practiced by Iona Thomas, Laura Lee, Pearl Harris Evans, and countless others, experienced its brief heyday during a time of great transition in the southeastern United States. The regional memorial traditions that generated an abundance of colorful ribbon, the experienced utility quilters who were not afraid to dirty their hands in order to "use everything for something," and the pervasive societal convention that equated a profusion of floral offerings with elevated social status, all converged, for a fleeting moment, to give rise to a unique form of memorial expression.[114] The funeral ribbon quilts created at this key juncture serve as tangible representations of the changing nature of death and life in the twentieth-century South.

Acknowledgments

The author gratefully acknowledges the many individuals who generously shared their quilts, memories, and time in the development of this paper. Tricia Blakistone facilitated social media contacts; Cathy East painstakingly copyedited a first draft; RaeLana Poteat offered thoughtful comments; Lynne Zacek Bassett skillfully guided the paper and the author through the publication process; and Laurel Horton provided helpful suggestions and contacts.

Notes and References

1. Janice Long, interviewed by Diana Bell-Kite, December 9, 2014, Raleigh, NC. Transcript, North Carolina Museum of History, (hereafter NCMOH) Raleigh, NC.

2. "North Carolina, Death Certificates, 1909–1975," (hereafter NCDC), Ancestry.com; entry for Claude Hallman Thomas, Lee Co., December 4, 1955, citing Death Certificate (hereafter DC) no. 30130, North Carolina State Board of Health, Bureau of Vital Statistics, (hereafter NCSBH, BVS) Raleigh, NC.

3. Iona McNeill Thomas, Funeral Ribbon Quilt, 1956, private collection.

4. This study focuses specifically on funeral ribbon quilting as a form of memorialization, though some women did collect ribbons from the graves of strangers or from cemetery refuse piles for quiltmaking. Cora Meek of Mattoon, Illinois, practiced this method of quilting. She collected and saved ribbons until she had enough for a quilt. Meek was the only non-Southerner this author identified as making funeral ribbon quilts, though her methodology and purpose diverged sharply from the Southern tradition. (Ten museums in the Northeast and Midwest were queried in an attempt to find other non-Southern funeral ribbon quilts, but none were found.) For more on her life and work, see Lis Akolnik, "Fancy Work: The Domestic Textiles of Cora Meek," *In'tuit* 4, no. 2 (Winter 1996): 4–5. In addition to quilts made from the ribbons of known decedents, Laura Lee also made quilts from gathered ribbons; see Mary Anne McDonald, "Symbols from Ribbons: Afro-American Funeral-Ribbon Quilts in Chatham County, North Carolina," in *Arts in Earnest: North Carolina Folklife,* ed. Daniel W. Patterson and Charles G. Zugg (Durham: Duke University Press, 1990), 175.

5. McDonald, "Symbols from Ribbons," 166, 176.

6. Ibid., 167.

7. Lynne Marrs Hammer Ferguson, "Where Have All The Flowers Gone: A Study of a Funeral Ribbon Quilt" (Folk Art and Technology Paper, Western Kentucky University, 2004), 20. http://digitalcommons.wku.edu/dlsc_fa_fin_aid/512/.

8. Ibid., 21.

9. Ibid., 19. Ferguson briefly mentions at the paper's conclusion that her paternal grandmother, Ella Hammer, also used funeral ribbons to make pillows. This suggests a more widespread tradition than even Ferguson's initial thesis implies.

10. Gail Andrews Trechsel, "Mourning Quilts in America," in *Uncoverings 1989*, ed. Laurel Horton (San Francisco: American Quilt Study Group,1990), 139.

11. Ibid., 151.

12. Ibid., 152.

13. Joyce Joines Newman, "Making Do," in *North Carolina Quilts,* ed. Ruth Haislip Roberson (Chapel Hill: University of North Carolina Press, 1988), 33.

14. Cuesta Benberry, *A Piece of My Soul: Quilts by Black Arkansans* (Fayetteville: University of Arkansas Press, 2000), 47.

15. For the purposes of this study, the "South" is defined as the cultural region south of the Mason-Dixon Line and Ohio River, as well as and including all states that joined the Confederacy during the Civil War.

16. Annie Vaughan, Ribbon Quilt, 1946, from NCMOH, North Carolina Quilt Project (hereafter NCQP), published in *The Quilt Index,* http://www.quiltindex.org/fulldisplay. php?kid=4B-82-B41. Roger Hux, February 4, 2016, personal email message, February 5, 2016). The 1984 Hux quilt appears to be an outlier in terms of date. It is the latest in the sample by ten years. The next-latest quilt, also made by Hux, dates to 1974. All of the others studied fall within the 1946–1974 span.

17. For more on mourning quilts, see: Carol Williams Gebel, "Quilts in the Final Rite of Passage: A Multicultural Study," *Uncoverings* 16 (1995): 199–227; Elise Schebler Roberts, *The Quilt: A History and Celebration of an American Art Form* (St. Paul: Voyager Press, 2007), 133–143; Patsy and Myron Orlofsky, *Quilts in America* (New York: McGraw-Hill, 1974), 226–227; Roderick Kiracofe, *The American Quilt: A History of Cloth and Comfort 1750–1950* (New York: Clarkson Potter, 1993), 170–171.

18. See Gary Laderman, *The Sacred Remains: American Attitudes Toward Death, 1799–1883* (New Haven: Yale University Press, 1999); James J. Farrell, *Inventing the American Way of Death, 1830–1920* (Philadelphia: Temple University Press, 1980); and Drew Gilpin Faust, *This Republic of Suffering: Death and the American Civil War* (New York: Knopf Doubleday Publishing Group, 2008).

19. Gary Laderman, *Rest in Peace: A Cultural History of Death and the Funeral Home in Twentieth-Century America* (New York: Oxford University Press, 2003), 4.

20. Ibid., 16.

21. Charles Reagan Wilson, "Funerals," in *Encyclopedia of Southern Culture,* ed. Charles Reagan Wilson and William Ferris (Chapel Hill: University of North Carolina Press, 1989), 479.

22. Ibid., 479.

23. Laderman, *The Sacred Remains,* 152.

24. Stanley B. Burns, *Sleeping Beauty: Memorial Photography in America* (Pasadena: Twelvetree Press, 1990), "A Chronology, 1949."

25. Charles Reagan Wilson, "The Southern Funeral Director: Managing Death in the New South," *Georgia Historical Quarterly* 67, no. 1 (1983): 50.

26. Ibid., 51.

27. In a random sampling of fifty death certificates from North Carolina in 1955 and fifty from Pennsylvania that same year, the average time span between death and burial was two days in North Carolina and three and a half in Pennsylvania, "NCDC, 1909–1975," Ancestry.com; NCSBH, BVS, Raleigh, North Carolina; "Pennsylvania, Death Certificates, 1906–1963," (hereafter PDC) Ancestry.com, Commonwealth of Pennsylvania Department of Health and Vital Statistics, (hereafter CPDHVS), Harrisburg, Pennsylvania.

28. Gary Laderman, "Funeral Industry" in *Encyclopedia of Death and Dying,*

www.deathreference.com/En-Gh/Funeral-Industry.html.

29. Burns, *Sleeping Beauty,* pl. 64.

30. Leon J. Tolle Jr., *Floral Art for Religious Events: A Definitive Manual of Tradition and Design for Worship, Weddings, Funerals and Other Occasions* (New York: Hearthside Press, 1969), 175.

31. Burns, *Sleeping Beauty,* "Death in America: A Chronology, 1960."

32. Robert H. Brown, "Alabama Nostalgia," *Southern Florist & Nurseryman* 86, no. 8 (April 22, 1973): 19.

33. Ibid.

34. *Florists' Review,* 114 (April 1, 1954): 100.

35. "Tar Heels at Pinehurst," *Florists' Review* 115 (October 14, 1954): 22.

36. Brown, "Alabama Nostalgia," 18.

37. Georgia Effertz, "Funeral Flowers," *Southern Florist & Nurseryman* 85, no. 41 (January 12, 1973): 25.

38. Michael Trogdon, telephone interview by author, April 10, 2015.

39. Effertz, "Funeral Flowers," 25.

40. Joseph J. Pizzuto, *Fabric Science,* 5th ed. (New York: Fairchild Publications, 1990), 37.

41. Brown, "Alabama Nostalgia," 19.

42. Trogdon interview; Phyllis G. Tortora, ed., *Fairchild's Dictionary of Textiles,* 7th ed. (New York: Fairchild Publications, 1996), 343.

43. Pizzuto, "Fabric Science," 37. Until 1953, when the US Federal Trade Commission required that acetate be labeled distinctly from rayon, the two materials were considered to be the same fabric.

44. Christopher Crocker, "The Southern Way of Death," in *The Not So Solid South: Anthropological Studies in a Regional Subculture,* ed. J. Kenneth Morland (Athens: University of Georgia Press, 1971): 122.

45. Ibid.

46. Effertz, "Funeral Flowers," 25.

47. Ibid.

48. Ibid.

49. Trogdon interview; Effertz, "Funeral Flowers," 25.

50. Lynn Sanders Wilkinson, personal email message, April 9, 2015.

51. Ferguson, "Where Have All the Flowers Gone," 5.

52. Trogdon interview.

53. Ibid.

54. Joyce Robinson Broyles, telephone interview by author, November 21, 2014.

55. Crocker, "Southern Way of Death," 123; Amanda Greene, "The flower child: It's a tradition many have forgotten, but the spirit of young girls bringing bouquets to the dead lives on in a few congregations," StarNewsOnline.com, July 29, 2006, www.starnewsonline.com/article/20060729/NEWS/607290340?template=printpicart.

56. 1940 US Census, Population Schedule, Ancestry.com: Haywood County, NC, Crabtree, sheet 12B, household 184, Susie Neland; Stanly, NC, Tyson, 12A, 175, Vera Morris; Randolph, NC, Franklinville, 4A, 72, Mary L. Trogdon; Monroe, KY, Magistral District #6, 2B, 35, Roxy Hale; Chatham, NC, Oakland, 3A, 35, Laura Lee; Mercer, WV, Rock, 20A, 307, Sadie Cook; Walker, AL, Precinct 12, 16B, Bessie Alexander; Bell, KY, Middleboro, 15A, 258, Mattie Parr; Roane, TN, Civil District 1, 12A, Maddie E Robinson; Lee, NC, Cape Fear, 3A,

Iola Thomas,; Coffee, AL, E.P. 3, 2A, Annie L. Vaughan; Emanuel, GA, MD/560 District, 2B, Blanche Parham.

57. Ibid.

58. Mary Clement Allen, telephone interview by author, November 17, 2014.

59. Vaughan, Ribbon Quilt, 1946; Annie Vaughan, Ribbon Quilt, 1954, From NCMOH, NCQP, Published in *The Quilt Index,* www.quiltindex.org/fulldisplay.php?kid=4B-82-EAB.

60. Ruth Moose, personal email message, April 2, 2015.

61. Ibid.

62. Allen interview.

63. "United States Social Security Death Index," (hereafter USSSDI) Ancestry.com, Vera S. Morris, June 13, 1998, citing U.S. Social Security Administration, *Death Master File,* Social Security Administration (hereafter USSSA, DMF, SSA); "NCDC, 1909–1975," Ancestry.com, entry for Ardie Lloyd Morris, Stanly, March 19, 1971, citing DC no. 10846, NCSBH, BVS, Raleigh, North Carolina; Moose email; "NCDC, 1909–1975," Ancestry.com, entry for Iona McNeill Thomas, Lee, January 12, 1969, citing DC no. 2431, NCSBH, BVS, Raleigh, North Carolina; "NCDC, 1909–1975," Ancestry.com, Thomas DC; Long oral history; "USSSDI," Ancestry.com, Mary C. Trogdon, April 10, 1990, citing USSSA, *DMF,* SSA; "NCDC, 1909–1975," Ancestry.com, entry for Robert Ferree Trogdon, Randolph, May 2, 1953, citing DC no. 12486, NCSBH, BVS, Raleigh, North Carolina; Trogdon interview; Ferguson, "Where Have All The Flowers Gone," 10–13; "USSSDI," Ancestry.com, Pearl Evans, November 1985, citing USSSA, *DMF,* SSA; "USSSDI," Ancestry.com, Blanche L. Hux, 9 December 2012, citing USSSA, *DMF,* SSA; "NCDC, 1909–1975," Ancestry.com, entry for Willie Raymond Riggan, Warren, May 30, 1951, citing DC no. 15027, NCSBH, BVS, Raleigh, North Carolina; Pearl Evans, Unknown, 1958, From NCMOH, NCQP, Published in *The Quilt Index,* www.quiltindex.org/fulldisplay.php?kid=4B-82-D9D; McDonald, "Symbols from Ribbons," 173–175; "USSSDI," Ancestry.com, Susie McKnight, December 1983, citing USSSA, DMF, SSA; "NCDC, 1909–1975," Ancestry.com, entry for Myrtle Ferguson Webb, Cumberland, January 29, 1963, citing DC no. 767, NCSBH, BVS, Raleigh, North Carolina; Allen interview; "Madie Robinson," Piney Grove Cemetery, Midtown, Roane, Tennessee, Findagrave.com; "Tennessee, Death Records, 1908–1958," (hereafter TDR) Ancestry.com, entry for John Robinson, Roane, January 30, 1958, citing DC no. 58-1813, Tennessee Department of Public Health, Division of Vital Statistics, (hereafter TDPH, DVS), Nashville, Tennessee; "Mattie Parr," Piney Grove Cemetery, Midtown, Roane, Tennessee, Findagrave.com; "TDR 1908–1958," Ancestry.com, entry for Mildred Lois Kelly, Roane, July 10, 1948, citing DC no. 15723, TDPH, DVS, Nashville, Tennessee; Broyles interview; "USSSDI," Ancestry.com, Sadie H. Cook, June 6, 1994, citing USSSA, *DMF,* SSA; "Edward H. Cook," Burton Cemetery, Piedmont, Mercer, West Virginia, Findagrave.com; Sadie Cook, Ribbon Quilt, 1930 (date assigned by quilt search, ca. 1958 would be more accurate based on the date that Edward Hamilton Cook died), from West Virginia Department of Archives and History, West Virginia Heritage Quilt Search, Published in *The Quilt Index,* www.quiltindex.org/fulldisplay.php?kid=50-8A-732; "USSSDI," Ancestry.com, Annie L. Vaughan, February 25, 1993, citing USSSA, DMF, SSA; "Mary Jane Phillips Veal," Pleasant Ridge Cemetery, Arguta, Dale, Alabama, Findagrave.com; "Debbie Gail Warrick," Green Hills Memorial Cemetery, Pike, Alabama, Findagrave.com; Vaughan, Ribbon Quilt, 1946; Vaughan, Ribbon Quilt, 1954; "USSSDI," Ancestry.com, Bessie L. Alexander, February 13, 2006, citing USSSA, *DMF,* SSA; "USSSDI," Ancestry.com, Mary L. Alexander, April 15, 1972,

citing USSSA, *DMF,* SSA; Trechsel, "Mourning Quilts in America," 151–152.

64. Long oral history; Ferguson, "Where Have All the Flowers Gone," 13–14; McDonald, "Symbols from Ribbons," 170; Allen interview; Broyles interview.

65. See Robert Shaw, *American Quilts: The Democratic Art,* updated ed. (New York: Sterling, 2014), 277–307.

66. The ratios reflected in this sample should not be used as any sort of gauge of the relative popularity of funeral ribbon quilting among white women compared to black women or vice versa. The numbers presented likely reflect more about the author's own professional network and ability to make contact with various quilt owners than they do historical trends.

67. Diamond Star Quilt, 1959–1960, private collection; see Cuesta Benberry, *Always There: The African-American Presence in American Quilts,* (Louisville: The Kentucky Quilt Project, Inc., 1992); Shaw, *American Quilts,* 167–168.

68. Morris DC; Thomas DC; Trogdon DC; Riggan DC; Webb DC; Robinson DC; Kelly DC; Cook Grave; Veal Grave; Warrick Grave; Ferguson, "Where Have All The Flowers Gone," 10–13; McDonald, "Symbols from Ribbons," 173–175; USSSDI, Alexander; "PDC, 1906–1963," Ancestry.com, entry for Sylvester R. Goodwin, Tamaqua, November 15, 1959, citing DC no. 103686, CPDHVS, Harrisburg, Pennsylvania; "NCDC, 1909–1975," Ancestry.com, entry for Margaret Irene Wicker, Lee, February 19, 1958, citing DC no. 4610, NCSBH, BVS, Raleigh, North Carolina.

69. Pizzuto, "Fabric Science," 37.

70. Sherlie Hale Walker, quoted in Ferguson, "Where Have All The Flowers Gone," 14.

71. Allen interview.

72. Vaughan, Ribbon Quilt, 1946.

73. Cook, Ribbon Quilt, 1930/1958.

74. Funeral Ribbon Quilt, Sanford, North Carolina, 1958, private collection; Funeral Ribbon Quilt, Sanford, NC, 1958, collection of the NCMOH, accession 1993.221.1.

75. Funeral Ribbon Quilt, possibly AL, c. 1945–1975, collection of the National Museum of Funeral History, Houston, Texas.

76. Vaughan, Ribbon Quilt, 1946; Vaughan, Ribbon Quilt, 1954.

77. Evans, Unknown, 1958.

78. Linda Koehler, "Palmerton Library to host third annual Quilt Show," *Times News LLC,* October 8, 2009, www.tnonline.com/2009/oct/08/palmerton-library-host-third-annual-quilt-show; Darlene Risteter, telephone interview by author, February 11, 2015.

79. Trechsel, "Mourning Quilts in America," 152.

80. Central Medallion Quilt Top, Cotton Plant, AR, c. 1970, Old State House Museum, Little Rock, Arkansas, 1995.014.01.

81. Thomas, Funeral Ribbon Quilt, 1956.

82. Ferguson, "Where Have All the Flowers Gone," 6.

83. Ibid.

84. Trogdon interview.

85. Doris Ann Krupinski, "Design blueprint: Memory Picture," *Florists' Review* 149 (April 6, 1972): 57.

86. Vaughan, Ribbon Quilt, 1946; Vaughan, Ribbon Quilt, 1954.

87. Diamond Star Quilt, 1959–1960.

88. Cook, Ribbon Quilt, 1930/1958.

89. "Stitches in Time: 100 Years of Machines and Sewing," *Museum of American Heritage,* www.moah.org/stitches/index.html.

90. Funeral Ribbon Quilt, Sanford, North Carolina, 1958, private collection; Funeral Ribbon Quilt, Sanford, NC, 1958, NCMOH; Thomas, Funeral Ribbon Quilt, 1956; Moose email.

91. Evans, Unknown, 1958.

92. Ferguson, "Where Have All the Flowers Gone," 3, 5; Moose email.

93. See Gebel, "Quilts in the Final Rite of Passage," 199–227, for a more thorough examination of the psychological and physical roles quilts play in the grief process.

94. Crocker, "Southern Way of Death," 123.

95. Trechsel, "Mourning Quilts in America," 139.

96. Pizzuto, "Fabric Science," 37.

97. Ferguson, "Where Have All the Flowers Gone," 15.

98. Broyles interview.

99. Risteter interview.

100. Trogdon interview.

101. McDonald, "Symbols from Ribbons," 165.

102. Allen interview; Moose email.

103. Leslie Cox, interviewed by Diana Bell-Kite, December 9, 2014, Raleigh, North Carolina. Transcript, NCMOH, Raleigh, North Carolina.

104. Ruth Moose, "The Wreath-Ribbon Quilt," in Ruth Moose, *The Wreath Ribbon Quilt and Other Stories,* (Laurinburg, NC: St. Andrews Press, 1987), 64.

105. Laderman, *Rest in Peace,* xxi.

106. Jessica Mitford, *The American Way of Death* (New York: Simon and Schuster, 1963).

107. Laderman, *Rest in Peace,* xxi.

108. Mitford, *The American Way of Death,* 96.

109. Ibid., 110–122.

110. Georgia Effertz, "Groups Must Unify to Fight the Spread of 'Please Omit' Notices," *Southern Florist & Nurseryman* 85, no. 42 (January 19, 1973): 20.

111. "Leaflet promotes sympathy flowers," in *Southern Florist & Nurseryman* 86, no. 14 (June 1, 1973): 40.

112. Ibid., 42.

113. A select few florists probably continued using acetate ribbon after the early 1970s. The latest quilt considered in this sample was made in 1984, a decade later than any of the others studied. The florist in the small town of Twin City, Georgia, where E. Hugh Hux's funeral was held may have been an old-timer who chose not to adapt to newer materials. Hux email.

114. Vaughan, Ribbon Quilt, 1946.

Why Ernest Haight Made Quilts

Jonathan Gregory

In 1934, following a decade of personal losses and financial reversal, Ernest B. Haight (1899–1992) began quiltmaking, which he continued for the remainder of his productive years. As one who by nature and training focused on the process of making things as well as the aesthetics of what he made, Haight developed sew-then-cut and machine quilting approaches that increased the accuracy and efficiency of his quiltmaking. Quiltmaking fed his soul by providing a creative and practical activity that also satisfied his need for intellectual challenge, helped him cope with difficult circumstances and losses, and offered opportunities to serve others through generously sharing his quilts and quiltmaking practices. Quiltmakers recognized Haight's accomplishments during the 1970s' Quilt Revival; however the importance of quiltmaking to himself exceeded his influence on the direction of quiltmaking during the early years of the Revival

Introduction and Context

Ernest Byron Haight was born at home near David City, Nebraska, on July 20, 1899, the oldest of three sons of Elmer Wallace (E.W.) (1862–1944) and Flora Burr Haight (1876–1967).[1] He attended schools in Butler County, Nebraska, and earned Arts & Sciences and Agricultural Engineering degrees at the University of Nebraska in Lincoln in 1923 and 1924, respectively. Following graduation, Ernest returned to Eldorado, a working farm and dairy his paternal grandparents and great-uncle established on land they homesteaded in 1871, where he labored for the rest of his working days. He married Amelia Isabelle Hooper (1900-1995) on August 28, 1928. Together they raised five children—Aubrey, Mae Belle, Wallace, Elmer, and Mary—while also being active in the David City Baptist

Church and in other religious, charitable, agricultural, and civic organizations (fig. 1).

In the mid-1930s, Ernest began to make quilts using a treadle sewing machine and eventually worked on more than 400 of them over a fifty-year period. Early in his quiltmaking hobby, he developed timesaving, sew-then-cut piecing methods, which he used regularly in his original designs or adaptations of traditional and published patterns. Before his death, E. W. hand quilted the first eight of Ernest's machine-pieced quilts. Flora then became the primary hand quilter for the next fifteen years. Thereafter, Isabelle hand quilted several of Ernest's quilts made as wedding gifts for their children and for her to enter in the hand-quilting classes at the Butler County and Nebraska State Fairs. However, she was unable to keep up with how rapidly Ernest designed and machine pieced new tops. In the late 1950s, Ernest developed an efficient machine-quilting approach that enabled him to quilt one of his tops in about eight hours; he used this approach for the majority of the quilts he pieced during the next twenty-five years.

Ernest entered his original and precisely-made quilts in the Butler County and Nebraska State Fairs, where they regularly earned prizes. In 1974, he self-published his sew-then-cut and machine-quilting techniques in *Practical Machine-Quilting for the Home Maker*, and during the 1970s he regularly presented his quilts and techniques to women's clubs and quilt guilds in Nebraska.[2] His quilt designs and quiltmaking shortcuts had little direct impact on the 1970–1980s Quilt Revival because his age and Isabelle's blindness prevented him from taking the opportunities to develop a nationwide teaching, speaking, and writing business.[3] In 1986, the Nebraska State Quilt Guild inducted Ernest into the Nebraska Quilters Hall of Fame in recognition of his contributions to Nebraska quiltmaking. Ernest died on April 24, 1992, at David City.

Ernest was among a small group of men who quilted in the twentieth century prior to 1970. However, not much is known about them. Their novelty landed them in brief newspaper articles during the 1930s through the 1950s acclaiming their accomplishments, such as making many quilts, sewing quilts with a multitude of pieces, or winning contests or prizes. Identical articles appeared in multiple newspapers indicating that a news service syndicated the articles.[4] In addition, male quiltmakers received mention in newspapers published in the Great Plains during the second quarter of the twentieth century for participating in newspaper-sponsored contests. From 1931 through 1940, the Omaha *World Herald* sponsored

Fig. 1. Ernest B. Haight and family, c. 1950. From left to right: Wallace G., Ernest B., Elmer W., Mary E., Isabelle H., Aubrey E., and Mae Belle F. Haight. Wallace G. and Elizabeth W. Haight Family Personal Collection. Photograph by Boston Studio, David City, Nebraska.

quilt contests, in which some males participated, to promote the syndicated quilt pattern series it regularly published. Jan Stehlik, who studied the Omaha newspaper's contests, noted as examples that a paralyzed boy entered the 1934 contest, and a man who viewed the display of the 1934 contest's entries entered the following year's contest because he decided he could quilt as well as a woman. Stehlik concluded from the newspaper's descriptions of the many men who attended the contest exhibitions and the entries made by men and boys that "the quilt bug had bitten men and women."[5]

Evidence, therefore, indicates that men made quilts during the twentieth century, but as a topic of scholarly inquiry, male quiltmaking during the time period is an under-studied topic.[6] Even more obscure are works, scholarly or popular, that establish the reasons males make quilts. In the catalog accompanying the Shelburne Museum's 2012 exhibition "Man-Made Quilts: Civil War to the Present," Jean Burks, curator, noted some themes common to quilts made by men: "man-made quilts preserve important public and private events, express personal protest, or project the profession or passions of the makers."[7] Burks's statement is probably accurate, but it does not distinguish men's reasons for quiltmaking from women's; women share these motivations for quiltmaking. Joe Cunningham, writing in the same catalog, adds that men and boys have taken up quiltmaking when illnesses or disabilities have prevented them from performing other labor, in a "spirit of competition" with women, to answer an inner challenge, or as a means of earning income.[8] Even this list includes reasons that women make quilts. Whether men and women's reasons for quiltmaking are similar or distinctly different has not been established through research. Hopefully, though focused on only one individual, this essay about the reasons Ernest Haight made quilts will provide a beginning into greater understanding of male quiltmaking during the twentieth century.

Questioning the Motivation

During the 1970s and 1980s, Ernest recounted on several occasions a story in which Isabelle challenged him to make a quilt and he felt obligated to undertake her challenge.[9] Sometime in the early 1930s, he had commented on a quilt pieced by Mrs. Queen, Isabelle's grandmother, that he observed Isabelle hand quilting. He had noticed that the pattern pieces didn't meet in sharp, precise corners. Trained in college to hold tolerances of 1/1000th of an inch, he felt justified in saying, "It looks like she could have done a better job." Isabelle replied, "Prove you can do better or keep still!"[10] This story is not substantial enough to explain fifty years of quiltmaking, however. Nor is it enough to account for why, as a practical man, he made more quilts than his family needed for warmth, why he made some of his most original quilts and set them aside for future weddings when he had three or four children to keep warm in unheated, upstairs bedrooms, why his most prolific season occurred after his children moved out, and why he worked on more than 400 quilts total. It also does not account for why he invested time in original designs and adaptations. Routinely entering quilts in the Butler County Fair and later in the Nebraska State Fair, and writing a booklet to demonstrate his efficient piecing and machine quilting techniques were not necessary to answer Isabelle's challenge. Ernest issued an open invitation to all interested persons to stop by Eldorado Farm and see his prize-winning quilts, accepted invitations to speak about and show quilts at quilt guilds, women's clubs, and church halls, and asked only that his hosts cover his expenses. He corresponded generously with anyone who inquired after quilting advice and instructions, but these behaviors were not required to prove he could accurately piece a quilt. He gave away nearly 120 quilts to charities, friends, and neighbors—gestures with no root in proving his abilities to anyone.

Why did Ernest invest so much of his time in quiltmaking? Isabelle, who was a regular diarist, wrote, "Daddy sewed on quilt," or, "Ernest sewing," or variations of the same hundreds of times in her quotidian writings.[11] Sometimes she was more efficient with her words, writing, "[Q]uilts of course," or "Ernest works on quilts constantly."[12] His quilt-making was so frequent that not sewing was worth exclaiming, "Ernest didn't sew today!!!"[13] What reasons explain the times he stayed up all night to quilt? Something else, something more propelled Ernest.

This essay considers the overarching question all the others posed above fit within: Why did Ernest make quilts? What follows considers how his quiltmaking coincided with significant life events and also examines the uses to which he put his quilts as avenues toward possible answers. The evidence suggests that Ernest made quilts for reasons that arose out of a series of losses, a need to escape or rest from the burden of his losses, a desire to use his natural endowments of creativity, intellect, and mechanical aptitudes that a sidelined engineering career left unexplored, and as a material legacy for his descendants. The evidence also indicates that, through quilts, Ernest had additional avenues to be productive and do something worthwhile as he grew older, and to be a good neighbor and live out his communitarian values. With quilts Ernest did good, both for himself and for others.

Coping and Being Himself

Ernest made one documented statement about the personal benefit he received from making quilts. It appears on a single day within Isabelle's forty-three years of daily diaries. "Ernest at work on quilts. He says he has to keep busy on [a] quilt to keep him from 'cracking up.' I know I do things like that too!"[14] "Cracking up" could mean anything from getting bored to having a psychological collapse. What he precisely meant and Isabelle understood is not revealed in the text. Ernest's actions, more than anything else, indicate that quiltmaking was important to him. Examining the circumstances surrounding the commencement of Ernest's quilt-making provides clues to his motivations.

Between 1923 and 1937, Ernest experienced a series of losses and reversals that left him with grief, thwarted aspirations, untapped potential, evaporated savings, and a heavy burden of responsibility to provide for his family during a drought and depressed economy. First, in 1923, during Ernest's years studying agricultural engineering at the University of Nebraska in Lincoln (1918–1924), his youngest brother Elton, age seventeen, drowned at a church youth group outing. Also, following the end of World War I, wheat prices plummeted, and the agricultural sector entered a depression that lasted until the beginning of World War II. Ernest was unable to find a job in agricultural engineering as a newly-minted graduate in January 1924. His father, E.W., was sixty-one when Ernest graduated and was nearing the age when he would need to hand care of Eldorado Farm, the family's 240 acres of farm and pasture land, to others. Ernest accepted the circumstances in which he found himself and returned to the farm, partly from necessity and partly from obligation, as a tenant who shared the income and expenses with his parents, who relocated to a house in David City.[15] His brother, Lewis, also returned to Eldorado for a few years, but left the partnership in 1932.

Ernest married eighteen-year-old Esther Ellender Guthrie in September 1926. She died, pregnant, less than six months later from complications of the flu and pre-eclampsia. He married again in August 1928, this time to Amelia Isabelle Hooper, daughter of the David City Baptist Church's new pastor. She was pregnant with their first son, Aubrey Ernest, when the stock market crashed in October 1929. Ernest and his father's invested profits from the farm evaporated with the collapse of the financial markets and the subsequent failure of their local bank through which they had made their investments. Once prosperous farmers, the Haights lost tens of thousands of dollars of accumulated wealth.[16] Persistent drought diminished their harvest yields in the 1930s. Drought denied any harvest in 1935 and 1936; grasshoppers ate most of the crops in the next growing cycle. In these low times, as his son Aubrey recalled, Ernest wept for his and his family's plight.[17] He and Isabelle continued as tenants on Eldorado Farm, meaning they paid two-fifths of everything gained as their rent for the property, further limiting their income from what little the land produced. When the crops failed, Ernest borrowed $1,000 without collateral from a David City bank to pay his bills and feed his family.

Taken altogether, Ernest had lost a brother, wife, child, hopes and aspirations, financial security, a source of income, and possibly his sense of agency as provider for his family. He had to puzzle through the resources and options available to solve or cope with these circumstances. Whether as a conscious choice or a serendipitous discovery, his beginning at quiltmaking in the mid 1930s coincided with what can only be described as the end of his rope.

From a practical viewpoint, quiltmaking gave Ernest agency once again to care for his family in their cold house and something to show for

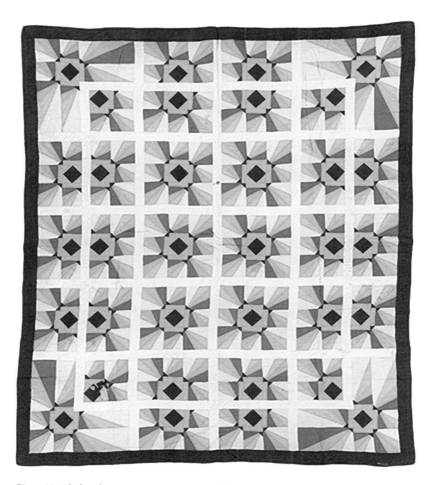

Fig. 2. Untitled quilt, c. 1935–1940. Private Collection. Image by the author and courtesy of the International Quilt Study Center & Museum.

his labor, unlike his work in the fields that proved to be "vanity and a striving after wind."[18] Considered more abstractly, Ernest's quilts were bright counterparts to the dreariness that afflicted much of the Great Plains during the 1930s. Quiltmaking ushered him into a bright place filled with clear colors of smooth, fresh cotton fabric, clean and unspotted. His quilts stood in contrast to the flyspecked, grasshopper eaten, grit-infused environment of the farm. When nothing grew and no amount of labor could coax an income from the soil or protect the crops from the jaws of the grasshopper, and when no rain meant no color sprouted from the soil, Ernest made quilts. When his family kept growing, but could not easily be fed, when the bank failed, and when he could not go on without crying, he made quilts. Whether consciously or not, he mirrored the complexity of his life in the complex geometry of his carefully drawn, exactly calculated angles (fig. 2). When the chaos of his life could not be assembled into a coherent reality, he chose orderly, repeating geometries in clear, solid hues and framing borders to control the composition. Imposing such order on his financial circumstances and governing agricultural outcomes were not nearly so attainable.

Ernest and Isabelle's children have come to see the existential benefits of quiltmaking throughout their father's lifetime. Youngest son, Elmer, expressed it this way:

Well, it was unusual [being a male quiltmaker], and he was able to make a mark, you know? I think I never was totally sure that he wanted, in the early years, anyhow, wanted to stay on the farm. I think he may have had aspirations to do something else. But the oldest son carried on the business. So he may have been looking for avenues to excel, you know, and he found one [in quiltmaking]." [19]

When reflecting on all that his father had lost between 1923 and 1937, and that his father spent the rest of his life recovering from the financial consequences in a career other than the one for which he had trained, Elmer said in a voice strained with emotion, "His quilt hobby was enormous. [Silence] Sort of a creative outlet you know."[20] Mary, the youngest child, described a transformation when her dad sewed, that he moved into a "zone." She noted that when he was in it, he stayed up late, suggesting that he enjoyed quilting as a restorative activity with benefits at least as valuable as the sleep would have been for him had he gone to bed.[21] Aubrey, the oldest Haight offspring, described the benefits of quiltmaking to his dad, also.

> Oh, yeah, [he quilted] every day. In the summer when things were really heavy with work, he didn't do much. . . . But he'd unwind, he'd come home after chores and milking cows, that's how he'd relax. He'd sit there at the sewing machine for a while and then go to bed. . . . He didn't do it from necessity. People did not need those quilts at that point. He was artistic. He had a sense of art, and he liked to do it. It was creative, and so that's what he did. That was his hobby.[22]

Fig. 3. *Blazing Star* quilt, 1935–36. Private Collection. Image by the author and courtesy of the International Quilt Study Center & Museum.

Peter Korn asks, "why do we choose the spiritually, emotionally, and physically demanding work of bringing new objects into the world with creativity and skill?"[23] He answers that, fundamentally, "we practice contemporary craft as a process of self-transformation." From his own experience as a maker of fine furniture, Korn knows that bringing something new and worth making into the world produces, as well, "the sense of meaning and fulfillment for which so many of us yearn so deeply."[24] Perhaps Ernest's quiltmaking was of this character, transporting himself from the burdens of his losses and the deficiencies of fulfillment in his career, into satisfying, meaningful, creative fulfillment. While making, he attained something closer to what it meant to be Ernest. Perhaps quilt-making made him feel more alive. To Ernest, quiltmaking was more than a means to an end; but, as asserted by Peter Dormer, "making is an end in itself."[25]

Validating his Creative and Intellectual Abilities

For many years Ernest experienced the personal benefits of his quilt-making. Making was its own reward and the quilts were useful and mean-ingful byproducts. At some point, however, Ernest began to wonder if what he made was good; at least, he was willing to let others see and evalu-ate his work. As one trained in the engineering profession, but who had not worked as an engineer, perhaps he sought validation of his creative and intellectual abilities as applied to quiltmaking. He participated in one of his community's mechanisms for discovering, assessing, and celebrating the skills and accomplishments of its inhabitants: the county fair.[26] In 1947 the Butler County Fair officials judged his and his father's Blazing Star quilt (fig. 3) as a prize example of the craft, an assessment that re-flected local values of what made a good quilt. Ernest's next documented prize-winning entry at the Butler County Fair was *Lone Star*, c. 1958, which he had machine pieced and his mother, Flora, had hand quilted.

Probably in 1959, Ernest submitted for the first time machine-quilted quilts to the Butler County Fair. As Ernest recounted in a 1984 letter, they were not welcome. "Finally I took some of my good-looking quilts to enter in our Butler County Fair, as machine-quilted. The Supt. of Needlework, looked them over, then declared that being machine-quilted, that was not 'Art,' and refused them. I took them home." For unknown reasons, Ernest was undeterred and tried again a year later. "The next year she said the same thing and refused them; but her assistant said to her, 'we have plenty of room to display them, and I think we should accept what ever [sic] is brought in, even if we have to make a special new classification. The Supt. just walked away, and the assistant made out the new entries. The judges immediately began to award them premiums."[27] A machine-quilted quilt, *Grandmother's Old-Fashioned Nosegay* quilt, earned a first premium in the 1960 Butler County Fair, the earliest documented entry of one of Ernest's machine-quilted quilts in a fair, and possibly the quilt in Ernest's account to his correspondent (fig. 4).[28]

Fig. 4. *Grandmother's Old-Fashioned Nosegay* quilt, c. 1960. Private Collection. Image by the author and courtesy of the International Quilt Study Center & Museum.

Ernest's sensibilities had been that machine quilting was suitable for utility quilts. But something shifted in his mind in the late 1950s when he determined that his machine quilting might be suitable for "fancy" quilts, i.e. those in which he also invested effort to create a pleasing design. Until this time, Flora or Isabelle had hand-quilted these decorative quilts for him, but they were not able to keep up with his production of machine-pieced quilt tops. He wrote, "By about 1960 we had quite a pile of un-quilted pieced quilt-tops. I had machine-quilted a few on our old foot-treadle sewing machine for our kids to use as they were growing up, and I found, as quilts wore out that the machine-stitched quilting seams would out-wear the fabric."[29] At this time, he started machine quilting his backlog of quilts that he had hoped to have hand quilted, and it was one of these that he attempted to enter in the 1959 Butler County Fair. Ernest pieced and his mother hand quilted a *Grandmother's Old-Fashioned Nosegay* quilt between 1957 and 1958 similar in size and colors to the machine-quilted *Grandmother's Old-Fashioned Nosegay* he entered in the 1960 Butler County Fair, verifying that the latter entry was of the type Ernest would have had hand quilted previously. His 1960 first-place ribbon on a machine-quilted quilt confirmed that his machine quilting designs and execution were judged appropriate for "fancy" work. For Ernest, the prize assessments for both his machine-pieced and hand-quilted quilts and those he made all by machine publicly validated what had before met his personal requirements of quality.

Later, in the 1960s, Ernest also submitted his quilts to the Nebraska State Fair and also won prizes. He earned his earliest documented State Fair ribbon in 1967 with the *Nebraska Centennial* quilt he machine pieced and Isabelle hand quilted. The following year, he entered a dark brown *Bachelor's Puzzle* quilt he had pieced and quilted by machine four years earlier, in 1964 (fig. 5). Possibly, he had hesitated to enter a machine-quilted piece at the state level until after he had received validation for a machine-pieced and hand-quilted one that conformed to quilt norms of the time. The Bachelor's Puzzle quilt earned a second prize, his first documented win at the state fair with a machine-quilted item. Thereafter, he annually entered several quilts in the Nebraska State Fair, some with Isabelle's hand quilting and others with his machine quilting. The judges consistently awarded him honors, many times first or second place.

As the Butler County Fair and the Nebraska State Fair each accepted Ernest's machine-quilted entries, they performed a process of shaping and reflecting community values in regard to quilts. Karal Ann Marling observed that at county fairs, the exhibits—and not the midway and entertainments—"are mostly about beauty and similar intangibles."[30] Fairs relate to everyday activities, but in a special local place, and the aesthetics of the everyday are judged by "subjective criteria of taste and superior powers of discernment" that both reflect and shape local values.[31] She writes: ". . . if neatly pieced quilts always take the prize over equally warm ones with stitches like hen tracks, a local standard begins to articulate itself and slowly influence the way future quilts will be made and appreci-

Fig. 5. Isabelle H. Haight and Ernest B. Haight with his machine-quilted Bachelor's Puzzle quilt at the 1968 Nebraska State Fair. Aubrey E. & Florence Haight Personal Collection.

ated. And so it goes for chocolate cake and dance steps, too. Beauty is in the eye of the beholder—the judge and, ultimately, the community."[32] Leslie Prosterman, another among the few scholars who have studied county fairs, noted that fairs perform for a community an ideal "world they would like to exist and highlights rules of conduct, sets of judgments, from which they know they deviate but which reinforce a sense of togetherness in a fractured and strife-ridden world."[33] Michael Marsden comments on this process and Prosterman's statements:

> "The process is not one of trying to achieve perfection, but rather one of trying to understand and apply the generally accepted standards by which to function well within the community. Yet within the frame of community standards, there is the spark of individuality that refuses to be sublimated and which, in turn,

fuels interest and excitement. Prosterman argues for the aesthetic values of the county fair this way: 'The fair is art: it showcases art, embodies aesthetic principles, and acts as forum for the development of aesthetics.'"[34]

When the Butler County Fairs' needlework assistant sidestepped the superintendent and accepted Ernest's machine-quilted entry in 1960, she was operating within this community process, validating his "spark of individuality." She gave the county's citizens something to talk about and evaluate themselves as part of the process of developing their community's standards of what was a good quilt.

With his community's validation, "prize-winning" became the way Ernest described his best quilts to others. When he introduced his quiltmaking in correspondence or public programs, he used the recognition of the fairs in his dossier of accomplishments.[35] He did not speak about the quality of his designs or color choices. He did not express his own confidence in the validity of the work, but he cited the Fair's assessment, revealing his belief that the Fair was authoritative on such matters, and verifying that he sought official approval of this cultural institution. With it, he crafted his own identity as a prize-winning quiltmaker. His prizes publicly and locally validated the worthiness of his craft. Nevertheless, Ernest's primary reasons for quiltmaking remained personal.

Growing Old and Leaving a Legacy

If quiltmaking provided a way to cope with difficulty and recover a sense of self in his middle years and to receive external validation of his creative and intellectual abilities, as Ernest aged, quiltmaking meaningfully filled in other areas of his life that were contracting. By 1960 his youngest child, Mary, was at the University of Nebraska, and others outside the family supplied more of the labor on Eldorado Farm. During these empty-nest years, Isabelle noted Ernest's more frequent quiltmaking. She mentioned Ernest's quilts by their pattern names and noted when he was drawing a new pattern, when he was lost in thought about a quilt idea, and comments about his processes. When he had the fewest family members to keep warm with bed quilts, he increased his quiltmaking. This increase coincided with a pivotal conversation about the future of Eldorado Farm that Ernest had with his youngest son, Elmer. By the summer of 1960, Aubrey and Wallace, the older sons, had each aimed

Fig. 6. *Martha Washington Star,* 1981. Private Collection. Image by the author and courtesy of the International Quilt Study Center & Museum.

themselves toward careers that interested them in machining and electronics, respectively. Elmer, after completing his military service, was poised to study civil engineering at the University of Nebraska in the fall. Ernest proposed to Elmer that if he were interested in taking over the farm, he would expand the farming operation by renting additional land

and begin the transition of Eldorado to the next generation. Elmer, as he thought his dad expected, declined the offer and explained that his intentions lay in engineering. Elmer understood that his opportunities for income would be limited at Eldorado since his grandmother Haight still owned the land—she owned it until Ernest and his younger brother Lewis each inherited portions upon her death in 1967; he didn't believe the farm could support his parents, grandmother, and the family he hoped to have. Elmer, today, believes that when he declined the offer to become a partner in the farm, his dad's interest in the farm diminished further.[36] As Ernest's attachment to the farm decreased, his productivity in quiltmaking increased. Between 1934 and 1959 Ernest made just forty-two quilts.[37] Between 1960 and 1964 he made twenty-six and between 1965 and 1969 he made sixty. His productivity increased further in the 1970s.

As Ernest aged, his quiltmaking changed character, too. As already noted, he placed more value on productivity as he grew older. Evidence from the quilts he made in the 1970s and later indicate that intellectual and creative stimulation might have become less important to him. In earlier years, he invested his best efforts in quilts he intended to enter in the county and state fairs. However, beginning in the 1970s, the quilts he made for these competitions displayed less pleasing color and fabric selection. In addition, he used less complex patterns and his accuracy in construction decreased. Also, he entered quilts he made for everyday use in the fair, and he did not attempt challenging original quilts any longer. He settled into using prints from his fabric stash, rather than purchasing solids for a specific quilt as he had done in the 1930s. Also, he opted for repeated blocks in which he had only to master one block, rather than manage a medallion design that covered the quilt top from edge to edge (see figures 3 and 6 for the contrast). He was simplifying. Overall, the quilts he made for fairs, for gifts, and for charity began to look more like each other. Not surprisingly, Ernest received fewer ribbons at the fairs and the ribbons he won were seldom first prize.[38]

Particularly after 1983, dementia factored into the changes in Ernest's quiltmaking and how he used the quilts. Ernest started giving away some of his prize-winning quilts made years earlier that he had reserved for his talks at clubs and guilds beginning in the 1970s. In the early 1980s, Ernest gave Margie Horacek, a volunteer for the Association for Retarded Citizens, Butler County, a red and white quilt that he told her he had specifically chosen for her organization's annual raffle. The quilt had received first place at the 1971 Nebraska State Fair.[39] Following a blackout and hospitalization in May 1984, Ernest attempted to give away some of Isabelle's hand-quilted quilts to people outside the family. Isabelle protested and he finally relented, but the episode upset her considerably.[40] As dementia increasingly veiled his personality and unraveled his social connections, his quiltmaking continued as a personal pursuit. Following his hospitalization in May 1984, rather than making a quilt for a gift or fair entry, he simply worked on a quilt. The thread of his quiltmaking time looped and tightened so that beginning and end met, knotted at the position of quiltmaking's fundamental benefit to him—making as a way to be himself.

The satisfaction of having sustained the hard work to recover from their financial reversal and the lengthy drought should have meant something to Ernest and Isabelle—and it likely did have its joys and satisfaction. Even though Ernest had come to own a share of Eldorado Farm after his mother's death in 1967, he had been certain since 1960 that the farm would eventually pass from the family, leaving no legacy in the land to another generation of Haights. Whether Ernest consciously chose quilts as his legacy to the next generations as early as 1960 is unknown, but commencing in 1966 and continuing each year through 1983 he gave a quilt he machine pieced and machine quilted to each of his children as a Christmas gift.[41] Ernest and Isabelle specially made or selected a completed quilt for each grandchild's birth. Ernest made a quilt for each grandchild's high school graduation and, prior to 1985, wedding. Each family, through these gifts and the quilts they acquired when Ernest and Isabelle's estate was dispersed in the mid-1990s, has a durable connection to their father, mother, and grandparents who each applied their minds and hands to making them.

By 1980, Ernest was conscious of his quilts amounting to a legacy for his family. One of Ernest's correspondents, Helen Ericson (owner of Mrs. Danner's Quilts in Emporia, Kansas) and her husband came "to see quilts" at Eldorado Farm on July 26, 1980. In the follow-up correspondence between them, he discussed the question of whether he sold his quilts. He explained the he did not want to sell his best quilts because, if he did, how could he and Isabelle ". . . show quilts that we no longer have? We expect any quilts left after we pass away to be divided among our 5 sons and daughters, and our grand children. I'm sure that will be a legacy that will be prized for many years."[42] Ernest's prediction was accurate; his descendants own over 200 quilts that he made or made together with his parents and Isabelle.[43]

Ernest's quiltmaking provided another legacy of sorts—this one consisting of his quiltmaking techniques he shared to the benefit of other quiltmakers. Paul Donovan, a quiltmaker from Houma, Louisiana, began a correspondence with Ernest in December 1977. Donovan, who had done all of his quiltmaking by hand to that point, was stymied with the inaccuracies of his quilt construction. He was frustrated with authors who emphasized accuracy in quilting but didn't share the processes to achieve it. He wrote to Ernest in hopes that the man who put "practical" in the title of his booklet might help him overcome the obstacles, which Ernest attempted to do. Through their brief period of correspondence the men developed an appreciation for each other. They exchanged two letters each, but Ernest declared Donovan a friend in that short time. Ernest wrote, "I consider you also a friend and a 'kindred' spirit, or I wouldn't spend all this time writing to you. . . . Come to think of it, life would be very dull indeed if we couldn't help each other at times and share experiences. This is the essence of civilization,—to help each other, especially the generations yet to come, to try to improve methods, situations, use of resources, etc., etc."[44]

Sharing and helping others had at some point entered into Ernest's world-view. His statement to Donovan echoes the ideals expressed by leaders in the field of engineering at the time Ernest was studying the subject at the university.[45] Providing practical and material aid to others is a core principle of Christian doctrine as well. As a follower of Jesus Christ, Ernest knew the essential Christian tenet of neighborly love: for example, in one of Jesus' parables, a Samaritan, an enemy of Jews, provided material aid to a Jewish man who had been beaten, robbed, and left to die along the highway.[46] Jesus used the story to illustrate that even one's enemy is their neighbor. When asked what was the greatest commandment, Jesus answered, "'Love the Lord your God with all your heart and with all your soul and with all your mind.' This is the first and greatest commandment. And the second is like it: 'Love your neighbor as yourself.' All the Law and the Prophets hang on these two commandments."[47] Ernest acted on his value of being a neighbor to others in need when, during the Great Depression, he hired unemployed men from David City for day labor at Eldorado Farm and fed them at his family's table, even though his own financial security was dubious. His son Aubrey remembered his dad defending his actions, arguing that these men had greater needs than his own.[48] Also, Ernest's son Elmer recalled that in the mid-1970s when his dad began to rent the farm to others, he chose a succession of tenants whose prior success at farming was below average. Elmer said his dad did it because he was generous and liked to help the "underdog."[49]

In addition to providing meaningful assistance to those in need throughout his life, Ernest invested his time and skill alongside many others in organizations necessary for his community's stability. He filled sustaining and maintaining roles in a number of civic, religious, political, and agricultural organizations. As examples, the East Olive Township, in which the Haights lived, had its own school. Those on the school board, of which Ernest was treasurer, repaired the buildings, shoveled the snow, and hired the teachers. Ernest shared responsibility in other organizations as well: he donated blood to and canvassed for the Red Cross, he served on the board of the East Olive Township Board, and filled an administrative role as treasurer of the York Baptist Association. He served the David City Baptist Church as treasurer, deacon, and Sunday School teacher; and he served as a Butler County election worker and as a Breeder's Association member. One might say that Ernest's life pattern was fulfilling roles that held civic and religious organizations together for the common good. He more likely thought of what he did as making sure his community had solid schools and churches, a strong agricultural economy and local government, and that those who were in need, near and far, were taken care of. These commitments assured continuation of a quality of life through sharing one's talents for the greater good of his "neighbors."

Ernest came to understand that he had something in his quiltmaking to share for the greater good as well. He generously gave away his quilts within a network of family and local relationships and organizations he valued. Ernest acknowledged, by giving a quilt to them, the important accomplishments in the lives of neighbors, Isabelle's piano students, and the David City Baptist Church congregants. He honored graduations, marriages, and births—all enrollments in the phases of life that lend stability to a place. He shared quilts with the residents of David Place and St. Joseph's Villa, the two retirement homes in David City, and, for approximately fifteen years, he donated quilts to the annual Association for Retarded Citizens, Butler County, raffle.[50] These gifts strengthened the bonds of family, friendship, and citizenship by supporting the well-being and growth of those within those circles. Ernest, with his gifts, signified his membership in these networks; his gifts were material reminders that the recipients belonged also. In these ways, Ernest's quilts represented his legacy as a meaningful and functioning member of his rural community.

In addition to giving quilts to others, Ernest came to understand that his knowledge about quiltmaking offered something of benefit to others who wanted to keep their families warm. Ernest's original, practical purpose for machine quilting in 1934 was to complete quilts his family needed for their beds. Likewise, he shared his methods from a desire to help others do the ordinary work of meeting their families' needs. He put it this way to Paul Donovan, ". . . fancy quilting patterns was not the primary reason why I experimented and developed my machine-quilting system. Most people do not make a quilt primarily for show or ornament but for practical use, but are stymied by the tremendous effort to hand-quilt it."[51] Ernest, with Isabelle at his side, shared these benefits repeatedly with small groups of women, donating their time and asking only for reimbursement of expenses. They packed their prize-winning quilts—reserved from daily use so they could be shown to others—into their car, and he used them to teach processes for making quilts for everyday use. He never ventured far, however, only traveling within a 100-mile radius of David City to speak and show his quilts (fig. 7).

When others outside his home community discovered his technical innovations in quiltmaking, Ernest chose not to take the opportunity to increase his income and broaden his influence, as other innovators were legitimately doing in the emerging quilt sector of the craft and hobby market. Instead, with his permission, others shared his techniques with the market. Bonnie Leman and Robbie Fanning both included his machine quilting process in "how-to" books written for quiltmakers.[52] He thought of these publications, and one he wrote and published himself, as a way to serve others. He said as much, repeatedly, in letters to his correspondents. To one he wrote:

"It was several years ago, after winning a number of premiums at our Nebraska State Fairs, the Superintendent of Needlework pressured me to publish a booklet to share with others how I do machine-quilting.[53] The original idea was to describe how the home-maker, after piecing her quilt, could rather quickly finish it in her own home, with her own hands, using equipment she already had or could borrow from quilt-making friends, e.g., the quilt frames I suggest to use in preparing the quilt for machine-quilting, and in a comparatively short time have a useful bed covering for her family to use. I had never planned to capitalize on this, but, primarily, just to share this information with others."[54]

Fig. 7. Ernest B. Haight demonstrating strip piecing at the Lincoln Quilters Guild Meeting, July 14, 1973. Image by Roger and Mary Ghormley. Image courtesy of Archives and Special Collections, University of Nebraska-Lincoln Libraries, Mary Ghormley Collection.

In *Practical Machine-Quilting for the Homemaker,* Ernest told the quiltmaker how to make conditions proper for machine quilting, even going so far as to provide a design for a quilting frame on which to layer the quilt and secure the layers together with safety pins before quilting. He included low- or no-cost suggestions, such as suggesting the use of a large piece of cardboard resting on the backs of dining chairs to extend the sewing table to hold the quilt as it was being quilted.[55]

Ernest's public engagement with others through his quiltmaking was of the same character as his involvements in family and community life. He simply extended the geography of his neighborhood to include all of eastern Nebraska and the readers of publications serving quiltmaking neighbors across the United States. For example, in a reply to a letter from Helen M. Ericson of Emporia, Kansas, he wrote, "We extend a most cordial invitation for you and some friends to come with you to see them [quilts], some time when you come to Lincoln."[56] Even in this instance he acted in a neighborly way, as if his correspondent was a next-door neighbor.

Ernest's actions revealed as clearly what he believed as did the philosophy he included in a letter to his nine-year-old granddaughter, Cheri, in 1970. She had asked him what life was like when he was her age. He told her that he did not have many of the conveniences she was familiar with: radio, television, car and air travel, paved roads, and electricity, among others. In spite of these things, he assured his granddaughter, life was good. "I believe people were probably as happy then as now, maybe even happier. Happiness may not consist of the abundance of things we have, but rather in the spirit of helpfulness to others, of being busy doing something worthwhile, and having a trust in the Heavenly Father . . ."[57]

Conclusion

Returning to the question raised at the beginning of this essay regarding the unique (or not) reasons for which men make quilts, Ernest's motivations for quiltmaking are harmonious with several of those observed by others. Through his quilts he recognized important private events in the lives of his family members and community. Additionally, his complex original designs reflected his professional training as an engineer. His quiltmaking was both in a spirit of competition with women (more accurately, to prove something to Isabelle) and to answer an inner challenge. This last reason, perhaps, is closest to the answer found in the many pieces of evidence provided by his quilts and the quiltmaking he carried on over five decades: Ernest made quilts because it allowed him to be himself.

At the beginning of his quiltmaking, his reasons were for the benefits that quiltmaking provided as an intermittent escape from the burdens he bore as a man experiencing significant personal and financial losses and as an outlet to exercise his intellectual and creative capacities. As the years passed, quiltmaking provided an opportunity to continue meaningful work into his last years of life. All of these benefits coalesced to provide self-discovery and fulfillment. Eventually, the quilts Ernest made—many of them made jointly with his father, mother, and wife—became the legacy he left his children. As a surprise to Ernest, what he pursued initially for his own benefit became a benefit to many others, too. He was unaware of quiltmakers' hunger for what he had learned about accurate and efficient quiltmaking, or that he had an opportunity to monetize his techniques. At the end of his life, Ernest expressed surprise, and an undertone of joy and satisfaction, at how much attention his quiltmaking had gathered. He wrote, "I had no idea this quilt venture would mushroom like it has."[58] He continued, "I had never planned to capitalize on this, but, primarily, just to share this information with others."[59] And that was what he did.

Acknowledgments

Funding for the research supporting this essay was provided in part by the Lincoln Quilters Guild, the Center for Great Plains Studies at the University of Nebraska-Lincoln, anonymously-funded graduate student research support funds for quilt study available through UNL, and financial and in-kind support from the author's family and friends. The International Quilt Study Center & Museum at UNL provided use of its photographic studio and other resources. The descendants of Ernest and Isabelle Haight generously shared their quilts, family papers, and friendship, without which this project could not have been successful.

Note

The author has included citations to diaries and correspondence written by Ernest B. Haight and Isabelle H. Haight that are in several personal collections and of oral interviews conducted by the author with the Haight children and grandchildren. To clarify in an individual reference which Haight family member wrote or spoke, the author has used the full name of each person in each note. However, the author has substituted abbreviations for Ernest Byron Haight (EBH) and Isabelle Hooper Haight (IHH) in the citations. For brevity, the author also has provided abbreviations for each personal collection that holds a source cited in this essay.

AUBHC, Aubrey E. & Florence Haight Personal Collection, Hudson, Iowa.
EILLC, Eileen M. Liebert Personal Collection, Mitchellville, Iowa.
ELMHC, Elmer W. & Darlene Haight and Family Personal Collection, Lakewood, Colorado.
WEHC, Wallace G. and Elizabeth W. Haight Family Personal Collection, Melbourne, Florida.

Notes and References

1. This essay, with modifications, was originally a chapter in the author's PhD dissertation. Jonathan Gregory, *Why Did Ernest Haight Make Quilts and Why Does It Matter?* (PhD diss., University of Nebraska-Lincoln, 2015).
2. EBH, *Practical Machine-Quilting for the Home Maker* (David City, NE: by the author), 1974.
3. For example, Hazel Carter invited Ernest to speak at the Continental Quilting Congress in 1979 or 1980. Carter had not thought about how old he was when she invited him. He replied, in a letter that Carter thought was "just so charming," that he was unable to accept the invitation. He had heard that the traffic was bad and that there was no way "this country boy" could undertake the trip. Hazel Carter, oral interview by the author at the American Quilt Study Group Seminar, Lincoln, Nebraska, October 6, 2012, notes in possession of the author.

4. In a search performed at Newspapers.com, on August 16, 2014, the author found at least twenty brief articles dated between 1922 and 1958, some duplicated in multiple newspapers, about male quilters. For example, "Finishes Quilt with 123,000 Pieces," *Santa Cruz [California] Sentinel,* December 20, 1950, and "Albert Makes His Quilt Masterpiece," *Gastonian [North Carolina] Gazette,* December 21, 1950, both report the completion by quiltmaker Albert Small, of Gastonia, Illinois, of a quilt comprised of a multitude of small pieces of fabric. Whereas the titles are different, the text of both articles is identical.

5. Jan Stehlik, "Quilt Patterns and Contests of the Omaha *World-Herald,* 1921–1941," in *Uncoverings 1990,* ed. Laurel Horton, vol. 11 (San Francisco, CA: American Quilt Study Group, 1991), 70.

6. The author was unable to identify scholarly sources that offered studies of individual male quiltmakers or examinations of particular questions about male quiltmakers, their quilts, and how gender factored into their quiltmaking choices. However, both popular and scholarly works exist that include basic biographical information about particular male quilters and descriptions of their quilts. See, for example, Florence Peto, *Historic Quilts* (New York: The American Historical Company, Inc., 1939), 115–136; Janet Carruth and Laurene Sinema, "Emma Andres and Her Six Grand Old Characters," in *Uncoverings 1990,* ed. Laurel Horton, vol. 11 (San Francisco: American Quilt Study Group, 1991), 88–108; and Jean M. Burks and Joe Cunningham, *Man-Made Quilts: Civil War to the Present* (Shelburne, Vt.: Shelburne Museum, 2012).

7. Burks and Cunningham, *Man-Made Quilts,* 1.

8. Ibid., 19–25.

9. Ernest recounted the story in his self-published booklet and in correspondence with quilters. See EBH, *Practical Machine-Quilting;* EBH, "Letter to Mrs. Carl Ewoldt," January 10, 1971, AUBHC; EBH, "Letter to Lillian G. Collins," April 21, 1981, EILLC. EBH's children also shared versions of the story in oral interviews with the author. See, for example, Aubrey E. Haight, Florence Haight, and Eileen Liebert, oral interview by the author, August 10, 2010, Hudson, Iowa; Mae Belle F. Haight, oral interview by the author, November 24, 2009, Lincoln, Nebraska.

10. EBH, "Letter to Lillian G. Collins;" EBH, "Letter to Paul M. Donovan," December 11, 1977, EILLC. Collins and her sister, Maurine Schuldt, from Caldwell, Idaho, purchased a quilt from Ernest in 1978. Donovan, a quiltmaker from Houma, Louisiana, wrote Ernest for advice on accurate piecing.

11. IHH, February 25, 1957, diary entry, 1955–1959 Five Year Diary, ELMHC; IHH, January 18, 1961, diary entry, 1960–1964 Five Year Diary, ELMHC.

12. IHH, February 3, 1961, diary entry, Ibid., ELMHC.; IHH, May 25, 1983, diary entry, 1983 Diary, ELMHC.

13. IHH, February 28, 1966, diary entry, 1966–1970 Fiver Year Diary, ELMHC.

14. IHH, March 1, 1962, journal entry, 1962 Journal, ELMHC

15. Ernest's obligation to return to Eldorado, the family farm, in 1924 is based on conversations with his son, Elmer W. Haight, who was offered, but declined, Ernest's offer to become a partner in the farm in about 1960. Elmer spoke of Ernest's feelings of obligation to his father in a 2010 interview, "I know that he felt responsible [to take over the farm]. He was the oldest son. Someone had to take over the farm and he accepted it." Elmer W. & Darlene Haight, oral interview by the author, July 18, 2010; Elmer W. Haight, telephone conversation with the author, January 31, 2015.

16. Aubrey E. Haight, Florence Haight, and Eileen Liebert, oral interview by the author. Aubrey Haight recalls that his grandfather, E.W. Haight, lost $50,000 and his father, Ernest, lost approximately $10,000. Adjusted for inflation, a $50,000 investment in 1929 is equivalent to approximately $700,000 in 2014 dollars. "Inflation Calculator: Bureau of Labor Statistics," http://www.bls.gov/data/inflation_calculator.htm.

17. Aubrey E. Haight, oral interview with the author, June 9, 2013, David City, Nebraska.

18. Eccles. 1:7 (English Standard Version).

19. Elmer W. & Darlene Haight, oral interview by the author, July 18, 2010, Lakewood, Colorado.

20. Elmer W. & Darlene Haight, oral interview by the author, March 31, 2014, Lakewood, Colorado.

21. Mary E. Haight, oral interview by the author, July 16, 2010, Greeley, Colorado.

22. Aubrey E. Haight, Florence Haight, and Eileen Liebert, oral interview with the author, August 10, 2010.

23. Peter Korn, *Why We Make Things and Why It Matters: The Education of a Craftsman* (Boston: David R. Godine, 2013), 7.

24. Ibid.

25. Quoted in David Gauntlett, *Making Is Connecting: The Social Meaning of Creativity, from DIY and Knitting to YouTube and Web 2.0* (Malden, MA: Polity Press, 2011), 25.

26. Leslie Mina Prosterman, *Ordinary Life, Festival Days: Aesthetics in the Midwestern County Fair* (Washington, D.C.: Smithsonian Institution Press, 1995). Prosterman describes how the processes of creating entry classes, community members' interpretations of those classes according to their own ideas and skills, and judges' assessments of entries are among the mechanisms for developing a community's aesthetics.

27. EBH, "Letter to Mrs. Betsy Faske," August 12, 1943, Harriet Hargrave personal collection.

28. EBH, *Grandmother's Old-Fashioned Nosegay,* color photographic print, October 1970, Aubrey E. & Florence Haight personal collection, Hudson, Iowa. Ernest hand inscribed the back of the photograph with the quilt's name, that it was machine-quilted, and that it received "1st, Butler Co. Fair 1960."

29. EBH, "Letter to Mrs. Betsy Faske."

30. Greta Pratt and Karal Ann Marling, "Fairs: A Fixed Point on the Turning Wheel of Time," *American Art* 7, no. 2 (April 1, 1993): 24.

31. Ibid.

32. Ibid.

33. Prosterman, *Ordinary Life, Festival Days,* 12.

34. Michael T. Marsden, "The County Fair as Celebration and Cultural Text," *The Journal of American Culture* 33, no. 1 (March 1, 2010): 27. Marsden provides an abbreviated historiography of county fairs studies, which references Prosterman's *Ordinary Life, Festival Days,* in his assessment of the 2008 and 2009 Brown County, Wisconsin, Fair. See also Prosterman, *Ordinary Life, Festival Days,* 198.

35. For example, see EBH, "Letter to Helen M. Ericson," August 28, 1980, EILLC.

36. Elmer W. Haight, telephone conversation with the author, January 31, 2015.

37. Though Ernest had done some machine quilting in the late 1940s, prior to 1961, when he "made" quilts, he machine pieced them and others hand quilted them. After Ernest purchased an electric sewing machine in 1961 and his mother, Flora Haight, who had hand

quilted for him, became ill and moved to a nursing home in 1962, Ernest machine pieced his quilts and, increasingly, machine quilted them also.

38. The author's assertion here is based on examination of more than 200 quilts made by Ernest over the fifty years during which he made quilts, and a large body of documentary evidence regarding the quilts and the prizes earned.

39. Margie Horacek, oral interview by the author, April 5, 2014, David City, Neb., April 5, 2014.

40. IHH, July 16, 1984, diary entry, 1984 Diary, ELMHC.

41. At Christmas 1984 and 1985, Ernest and Isabelle gave their children "prize-winning" quilts that Ernest had made or that they made together during the 1960s and 1970s.

42. IHH, July 26, 1980, diary entry, 1976–1980 Five Year Diary, ELMHC; EBH, "Letter to Helen M. Ericson."

43. The author, through physical examination of quilts in Haight family collections and perusal of primary documentary evidence, compiled a list of quilts made by Ernest and his immediate family. The list is included as an Appendix in the author's PhD dissertation. See Gregory, *"Why Did Ernest Haight Make Quilts and Why Does It Matter?"*

44. EBH, "Letter to Paul M. Donovan," December 22, 1977, EILLC.

45. See, for example, W. F. Durand, "The Engineer and Civilization," *Science* (December 11, 1925), 525–33; John J. Carty, "Ideals of the Engineer," *Science* (March 23, 1928), 307–9.

46. See Luke 10:25–37.

47. Matthew 22:37–40, New International Version, available at https://www.biblegateway.com/passage/?search=Matthew+22:36-40.

48. Aubrey E. Haight, Florence Haight, and Eileen Liebert, oral interview by the author.

49. Elmer W. Haight, telephone conversation with the author, January 31, 2015.

50. Ernest made forty-nine quilts for David City retirement homes, the Retarded Citizens Association, and other charities; and he made fifty-nine quilts as gifts on various occasions to members of the local community. He also made 160 quilts as gifts to family members.

51. EBH, "Letter to Paul M. Donovan," December 22, 1977.

52. Bonnie Leman, *Quick and Easy Quilting* (Great Neck, NY: Hearthside Press, 1972); Robbie Fanning and Tony Fanning, *The Complete Book of Machine Quilting* (Radnor, PA: Chilton Book Co., 1980).

53. Ernest was encouraged to publish his machine-quilting method by Louise Howey, who held many positions, including needlework superintendent, at the Nebraska State Fair between 1946 and 1984. See Patricia Cox Crews and Ronald C. Naugle, *Nebraska Quilts & Quiltmakers* (Lincoln: University of Nebraska Press, 1991), 222.

54. Copies survive of four letters in which Ernest wrote nearly identical descriptions of his reasons to publish his book. The quoted section is from his letter to Helen Ericson. EBH, "Letter to Paul M. Donovan," December 22, 1977; EBH, "Letter to Nadine Berthold," August 5, 1978, EILLC; EBH, "Letter to Helen M. Ericson;" EBH, "Letter to Mrs. Roman Turck," October 31, 1981, EILLC.

55. EBH, *Practical Machine Quilting.*

56. EBH, "Letter to Helen M. Ericson."

57. EBH, "Letter to Cheri Haight," August 14, 1970, WEHC.

58. EBH, "Letter to Nadine Berthold."

59. EBH, "Letter to Helen M. Ericson."

The Godey Quilt:
One Woman's Dream Becomes a Reality

Sandra Staebell

The Godey Quilt *is a 1930s appliqué quilt composed of fifteen fabric portraits of men and women clothed in fashionable mid-nineteenth century attire. The dream of Mildred Potter Lissauer (1897–1998) of Louisville, Kentucky, this textile is a largely original design that is not representative of the majority of American quilts made during the early 1930s. Notable for the beauty and quality of its workmanship, the quilt's crafting was, in part, a response to the competitive spirit that reigned in quiltmaking at the time. Significantly, the survival of the materials that document its conception, design, and construction enhances its significance and can be used to create a timeline of its creation. Reflecting Colonial Revival concepts and imagery, the* Godey Quilt *is a remarkable physical expression of that era.*

Introduction

"Masterpiece" is a sometimes undeserved accolade, but in the case of the *Godey Quilt,* the description fits (fig.1). Begun in 1933 and completed the following year, it was the work of a purportedly novice quilter, Mildred Potter Lissauer of Louisville, Kentucky. For nearly all Depression era quiltmakers, the act of creation was important, allowing them to display their "skill and ingenuity in the design and the quilting."[1] Yet, in many ways the *Godey Quilt* is uncharacteristic of the majority of quilts that date from the early 1930s. Unlike so many of her fellow quilters, Lissauer was a well-to-do Southerner who made her quilt solely for artistic and personal reasons. Not only that, the *Godey Quilt* was based on a largely original design during a time when patterns and kit quilts were widely available, promoted, and accepted. As a result, it had little in common with the majority of quilts from the period.

Highly publicized precedents for pictorial quilts composed chiefly of

Fig. 1. Mildred Potter Lissauer, *Godey Quilt*, 1933–1934. 102 x 91 3/4 inches. Kentucky Museum, Western Kentucky University (WKU), 1990.6.1.

figural elements existed in the 1920s and 1930s. Charles Pratt received acclaim for a series of pictorial quilts that included *Penn's Treaty* (1926) and *Ruth and Naomi* (1930); his work in turn influenced Emma Andres, whose *Lady at the Spinning Wheel* (1933) used 3,630 pieces of silk to depict one of the more recognizable images of the Colonial Revival era.[2] Several of the finalists in the 1933 Century of Progress Contest depicted American historical figures and events, including contestant Emma Mae Leonard who used eight figural blocks to illustrate a century of women's fashion in her entry, *1833-1933*.[3] Regrettably, the judges valued traditional patterns over originality, and only two of the commemoratives reached the finals.[4]

Researchers have studied quilts from this era at length, but the *Godey Quilt* provides a rare opportunity to analyze an exceptional quilt using the materials associated with its conception, design, and construction.[5] Rather than rely on period garments and images for inspiration, Lissauer adapted the romanticized images depicted on an extensive collection of printed materials, including newspaper and magazine advertisements and greeting and playing cards, for use as source material in drafting the appliqués on her quilt. Furthermore, fabric remnants left over from constructing the appliqués and foundation offer a rare opportunity for fiber analysis, and manuscript materials housed in Library Special Collections, Western Kentucky University (WKU) open a window into the quiltmaker's interactions with others during its creation and provide insight into her background and personality. Accounts from newspapers and magazines and historic photographs present additional sources of information about what happened to the quilt between its completion in 1934 and its donation to the Kentucky Museum at WKU in 1990.

Mildred Potter Lissauer

Lissauer was the second of four children born to William J. (1860–1952) and Martha Woods Potter (1868–1963) of Bowling Green, Kentucky. From an early age she demonstrated an interest in sewing and clothing, noting in later years that "even as a small girl my dolls had huge and elaborate wardrobes."[6] Mildred may have learned her sewing skills from her mother, a quilter who was appointed Warren County Home Decoration Agent in 1917, or her aunt, Mildred Woods Bagby (1868–1947), a prize-winning quilter in her own right. A second aunt, Elizabeth "Bethie" Woods (1865–1967), also quilted. While she was away at college, Lissauer garnered attention for her fashion sense and sewing skills. Potter described her daughter's appearance in a letter to her son:

> [Mildred] still paints her face, and wears the gaudiest colors. She wore a skirt of one color, and a waist of another, and shoes of another, and a hat of a thousand colors! . . . She says the teachers and every body [sic] at Cambridge told her she could make a fortune at dressmaking and designing. They paid her to copy some dresses she had made herself for them. . . . She is a case.[7]

Fig. 2. Mildred Potter Lissauer & Arthur Lissauer outside their residence in Louisville, Kentucky, 1930s. Courtesy of Department of Library Special Collections, WKU.

During the 1920s, Lissauer's social life included parties, golf matches, and dances. By 1923, her appearance appeared to comport more with her mother's sense of style. "Mildred came home on July 13th . . . she looks fine, a little thinner, and does not use any paint any more [sic], which improves her very much. She made some nice dresses and looks fine and stylish, as usual."[8]

Mildred's 1926 marriage to William R. Grace (b. 1881) ended in divorce three years later, but her 1931 nuptials with Louisville, Kentucky, businessman Arthur "Artie" Lissauer (1888–1973) proved a success (fig. 2). Known to their social set as the "Duke and Duchess," the couple entertained frequently at their Louisville home, "Green Pastures," as well as at their second home, "Much Ado About Nothing," in Winter Park, Florida. In her later years, Lissauer's wardrobe included a fringed suede leather swimsuit embellished with rhinestones and feather boas that she color coordinated with the rooms in her Louisville residence.[9]

Lissauer received attention for her unique decorating style—cuspidors, halved and used as flower urns; a barn window repurposed as a picture frame; and cheese graters transformed into a chandelier.[10] Her pride and joy perhaps was the prize-winning *Godey Quilt*. Finished in 1934, Lissauer gave it a place of honor in her Louisville home—a pantry converted into a bedroom furnished with early American reproduction furniture and two recommended, if historically inaccurate, hooked rugs (fig. 3).

Fig. 3. *Godey Quilt* displayed in a bedroom in Green Pastures, Lissauer's Louisville home, ca. 1939. Courtesy of Department of Library Special Collections, WKU.

Looking back, the quiltmaker was an upper-middle-class Southerner who came of age as America entered the Roaring Twenties. In terms of dress, deportment, and economic and social values, this decade was the most modern of times; yet many Americans looked back to our nation's perceived colonial past. As part of this trend, newspapers and magazines promoted traditional handicrafts, and in response, many women took up quiltmaking.[11] What attraction did the craft hold for an ostensibly modern woman like Lissauer? The editors of *Needlecraft* offered one explanation:

> Today's daughter may know her golf and her gears, her politics and her bridge, but she still proudly sews her fine seam. Her quilts are no longer just "comforters," household economies, they are made for their decorative value, and for the sheer joy of building beauty with a woman's tools.[12]

To understand why Lissauer made the *Godey Quilt,* it is necessary to understand the time in which she lived—the Colonial Revival era.

Colonial Revival Era

Exactly when did the Colonial Revival era happen? Early in the nineteenth century, the Picturesque movement praised the "simplicity and solidity" and "smallness and lowness" of many eighteenth-century structures.[13] Later on, widespread social, economic, and industrial changes in the United States during and after the Civil War caused many Americans to regard pre-1850s America as a "romanticized pre-industrial world of diligent, skilled, and contented workers—a world very different from that of the Colonial Revivalists themselves, with its troublesome issues of urban growth and shifting social patterns."[14] Some historians trace its beginnings to the Sanitary Fairs held to raise funds during the Civil War; many others believe that the Colonial Revival was an outgrowth of patriotic sentiments raised during the Philadelphia Centennial Exposition of 1876; and still others note the impact of the faux colonial architecture erected for the 1893 Columbian Exposition.[15] Yearning for a time when society was more homogeneous, gender roles seemingly well-defined, and the economic climate more secure, many Americans sought comfort in the past by joining newly formed lineage-based organizations like the National Society of the Sons of the American Revolution (established 1889), the National Society of the Daughters of the American Revolution (established 1890) and the National Society of the Colonial Dames (established 1891).

Many Americans held centennial teas, balls, and historical pageants, erected homes whose architecture reflected colonial themes, and/or furnished their interior spaces in the colonial style. Most did so, however, with little concern for historical accuracy. "For decorating and dressing, whether for an event or one's colonial-style home, replicating the past was not necessary. Capturing the charm, visual appeal and spirit of the past was more important."[16]

Books and magazines suggested Americans take up traditional handicrafts. In 1920 the editors of *Modern Priscilla* promoted a plan developed by The Society for the Revival of Household Industries and Domestic Arts to train returning World War I veterans in the arts of "flax-growing, hand-spinning and weaving of flax and wool, also quilting, candle-making, tatting, and other crafts" and encouraged their readers to contact the magazine about donating unused spinning wheels, looms, and other textile equipment.[17]

Seven years later, interest in the Colonial Revival and associated handicrafts remained high.

> That 'everything colonial goes, nowadays' is not disputed . . . a most delightful atmosphere, redolent of the "good old colony days," may be easily bestowed on the modern guest-chamber by the deft-fingered homemaker who looks well to the ways of her needle.[18]

The covers of ladies' magazines frequently depicted women spinning, weaving, or embroidering in romanticized pre-Victorian settings. In promoting traditional crafts, these periodicals published, gave away, and/or sold needlework patterns, often depicting colonial themes, to current and potential subscribers. An offer in the July 1935 edition of *Needlecraft* was typical. Individuals who signed up for a two-year subscription received a hot iron transfer set that included sheets of initials and patterns for a five-piece bedroom set and for a twelve-piece living room set.[19]

Fresh approaches emerged in twentieth-century needlework. Designers incorporated new styles, like Art Nouveau and Art Deco, into many of their designs, and novel fabrics and untraditional colors became the norm.

. . . why should we always slavishly copy our grandmother's quilting patterns? Surely our twentieth century designer has as good a knowledge of color, a better understanding of our modern aversion to "plain sewing," and a whimsical and charming imagination which she dares to use even when working with so humble a medium as cotton cloth.[20]

Improvements in manufactured kits, including the color-coded stamping of patterns sold by the Rainbow Quilt Block Company, made it easier for inexperienced stitchers to give needlework a try.[21] Significantly, ladies' magazines did not critique kits as "paint-by-number" exercises as sometimes happened later in the twentieth century.[22] Rather, they conveyed a message of enthusiastic endorsement for kits in all categories of needlework. As a result, these crafts were subtly modernized, and it became easier for women of all educational and social levels to practice needle arts.

Quiltmaking was an ongoing topic within the broader discussion of women's needlework during the first three decades of the twentieth century. In 1915 Marie Webster wrote, "City women, surrounded by many enticing distractions, are turning more and more to patchwork as a fascinating yet nerve-soothing occupation."[23] This interest continued into the 1930s. "Day by day the beauty of Colonial America is making its way into the modern home, and nothing is more eagerly pursued today than the antique quilts—the bright colored bed coverings that were the pride of our Grandmothers. The modern woman is enjoying the thrill of creating these same beautiful patterns with her own hands."[24]

The boudoir look which began around 1910 also affected quilting trends. Associated with French designer Paul Poiret, boudoir fashion and furnishings consisted of clothing, quilts, and cushions made from luxurious fabrics that were often enhanced by the addition of monograms, crests, and elaborate, often trapunto, quilting designs.[25] In the 1920s and 1930s, they were typically made in cottage industries in the Upper South and Midwest.[26] The Wilkinson Quilt Company of Ligonier, Indiana, was perhaps the earliest concern to capitalize on this trend with marketing that used phrases like "wonder-quilt," "exclusive design," and "Milady never tires of her Wilkinson Art Quilts."[27] In addition to whole-cloth quilts, these firms included appliqué quilts in their product lines.

Women could sew their own boudoir furnishings and attire, also. In September 1929 *Needlecraft* informed its readers that a set of six cushions would "make charming boudoir-pillows."[28] Fifteen months later, it promoted a "Trio of Sachets, Tuck-in-Pillow, and Dainty Lounging Coat," all of which were made using Italian quilting or "trapunto."[29] In 1931, kits for a "Heart-shape boudoir pillow" and a "Square boudoir pillow" underscored the continuing interest in the look.[30]

Lissauer was undoubtedly aware of these and other contemporary trends. She saved clippings from *Vogue* and *Needlecraft,* and family photos document a wardrobe that was not that of a woman scraping by during the Depression. Her social circle and proximity to the nearby Eleanor Beard Studio in Hardinsburg, Kentucky, make it probable that she was aware of the chic textiles it sold, as well as similar items marketed by competing concerns. Additionally, her mother's position as a county home extension agent implies some knowledge of current decorating trends. While there is no evidence that Lissauer was a quiltmaker prior to undertaking the *Godey Quilt,* her mother and aunts were experienced quilters, which likely piqued Lissauer's interest.

Inspiration and Influences

Why make the *Godey Quilt?* While earlier manuscript materials document an interest in sewing, taking on this particular challenge required Lissauer to compete in a sphere where her mother and aunts had considerably more experience. Family lore recalls that the *Godey Quilt* was the result of Lissauer's reaction to seeing a quilt made by a relative (fig. 4). Her first response was to remark, "I can do better than that."[31] Her second was to make the *Godey Quilt.* The likely inspiration was *Flower Baskets,* a quilt composed of ten baskets of two-toned pink and green flowers framed by an undulating swag-and-bud border, all appliquéd onto a pale oyster sateen foundation. Quilted in designs that include baskets of flowers and feather rosettes, it has the scalloped edge typical of appliqué quilts of this period. Who made it is unclear. One source identified Lissauer's aunt, Elizabeth "Bethie" Woods, while others attributed it to her mother or her Aunt Mildred Woods Bagby. Given the preponderance of manuscript evidence regarding her quiltmaking prowess, Bagby likely was the maker.

Stylistically, *Flower Baskets* dates from the late 1920s–early 1930s, but it is uncertain whether the design was original, based on a published pattern, or borrowed elements from two or more patterns. Similarities exist between this textile and other documented quilts of the period. Its swag-and-bud border treatment resembles that given to a *Rose of Sharon* quilt

Fig. 4. Attributed to Mildred Woods Bagby, *Flower Baskets* Quilt, late 1920s–early 1930s. 104 1/2 x 87 3/4 inches. Kentucky Museum, WKU, 1990.6.5.

advertised in catalogs published by the Wilkinson Quilt Company around 1916 and 1921 and one used for a *Forget-Me-Not* appliqué quilt marketed by Eleanor Beard.[32]

Several finalists in the 1933 Century of Progress Contest featured quilts made with undulating swag borders and similar color profiles. A comparison of Bagby's quilt with *Louisiana Rose* by Celia Pardue Hyde of Crowley, Louisiana, is instructive.[33] The color of the appliqué work and foundation of both quilts matches this period's preference for "plain colors, especially the 'boudoir shades—flesh, peach, apricot, pink, blue and orchid.'"[34] Both also include quilted motifs that mirror the outlines of each textile's respective appliqués, but Pardue handled the border in her quilt quite differently.

Mr. Godey's Ladies and Spinning Wheels

The *Godey Quilt* was named for the resemblance its appliqués bore to the fashion illustrations in the popular nineteenth-century ladies' magazine, *Godey's Lady's Book* (fig. 5). Published from 1830 to 1898, this magazine printed advice on home management, dressing fashionably, and rearing children; it also regularly included handwork projects. Fashion plate engravings, a feature of most contemporaneous women's magazines, became synonymous with Louis Godey's publication, and the phrase "Mr. Godey's ladies" entered the American vocabulary. Mildred's knowledge of these figures likely resulted from their widespread reproduction on a variety of printed media in the late 1920s and early 1930s; a June 1933 entry in her

Fig. 5. Fashion plate engraving from the September 1862 edition of *Godey's Lady's Book*. Courtesy of Department of Library Special Collections, WKU.

mother's journal states, "Mildred started her "Godey's Ladies.""[35]

Given that Lissauer almost certainly sought to make a quilt that was both familiar and unique, her decision to draw on Colonial Revival imagery in general and Godey-type figures in particular for its design is unsurprising. "Beginning in the early years of the century but especially in the interwar period—a time characterized by a general atmosphere of self-conscious modernism—popular needlework, perhaps more than any other type of graphic medium, was filled with images of a romanticized domestic past, including spinning wheels, cozy cottages, cheerful flower baskets, and happy women in hoopskirts."[36] During these interwar years, the figures depicted in household needlework were typically clothed in fashions that "functioned as symbolic two-dimensional versions of dress-up costumes."[37] Presented in romanticized settings or engaged in domestic or small group activities, the figures on the *Godey Quilt* mirrored the approach in colonial costuming that "portrayed a consistently gendered vision" that was "always disproportionately female-identified."[38]

Where did Lissauer find these images? Printed sources abounded. For starters, many pattern concerns used graphics of individuals clothed in "Early American" garb in their publications, and fictional characters, like Grandma Dexter and Grandmother Clark, became the corporate identity of thread, yarn, and pattern companies.[39] Locally, Louisville Bedding Company advertised its ready-made quilts using a catalog whose cover art was more Victorian than colonial in period.[40]

Godey prints were a popular home decorating motif, and Lissauer saved a promotion from *Woman's World Magazine* that informed subscribers they could purchase five such prints for fifty-five cents. The magazine deemed these pictures suitable for framing or for creating all manner of decorative objects including waste baskets, lampshades, and candy and cigar boxes.[41] In 1931, *Needlecraft* printed a feature promoting their use as lampshade embellishments.[42]

While no direct proof exists, a *Needlecraft* article, "Delightfully Quaint Bridge-Table Ensembles," likely influenced the design of the *Godey Quilt*. Published in October 1930, the similarities between one of its playing covers [table cloths] and refreshment cloths [napkins] and the *Godey Quilt* are noteworthy. First, the color of the foundation fabric recommended for the table cover, "Sateen in that shade of yellow-pink we know as peach" echoed the peach-colored "Buty Chine" that Lissauer chose for the foundation of her quilt.[43] Second, the instructions' call for solid-colored fabrics highlighted by embroidered accents mirrors some of the

Fig. 6. This playing card is part of a collection of materials that influenced the design of the *Godey Quilt.* Courtesy of Department of Library Special Collections, WKU.

Fig. 7. A magazine illustration inspired this sketch which Lissauer used for the design of figural appliqué Row 2, #3. Courtesy of Department of Library Special Collections, WKU.

choices Lissauer made. "The body of the bonnet is orchid, laid in solid rows of outline-stitch. There is a facing of delicate yellow, done in the same manner, close to the face, and trim and ties of similar color. . . . With a nosegay of French knots and daisy leaves the little figure is complete."[44] Third, the playing cover and two of Lissauer's appliqués included trellis-like effects, and fourth and finally, the editors of *Needlecraft* and Lissauer both displayed an awareness of the same deck of Godey playing cards. The former described the playing cover as "decorated to harmonize with the Godey ladies, Abigail and Melissa," and the latter saved nine playing cards whose backs were printed in one of three Lady Godey designs, including the two cards named in the article (fig. 6).[45]

One year later, this same magazine published a feature on four "Silhouetted Ladies," that Lissauer may also have seen.[46] Consisting of a handkerchief bag, cushion cover, hand towel, and tea cloth, it called for applying gingham cutouts onto the foundation and then adding embroidery highlights; this was simpler to make than the previous year's bridge table ensemble. The kits, which included hot-iron transfer pattern, perforated stamping pattern, stamped foundation fabric, appliqué material, piping or binding, and embroidery floss, cost from eighty cents for the cushion cover to $2.63 for the tea cloth.

Lissauer was familiar with the much-loved "Colonial Lady" motif. In its simplest form, it consisted of a woman depicted in profile dressed in a bonnet and oversize skirt and holding a parasol. *Colonial Lady Block 335* from the Rainbow Quilt Block Company was perhaps the most recognizable version, although many pattern companies published their own interpretations.[47] What were its origins? While some researchers suggest eighteenth- and nineteenth-century silhouettes as possible sources of inspirations, others have noted the appearance of the Sunbonnet Babies motif in 1900 and Marie Webster's *Keepsake Quilt* in 1912.[48]

A penciled notation indicates that Lissauer spent three hours a day for six months working on the appliqué designs. In developing her concept, she sketched approximately sixty figures onto paper, enlarging twenty-two of them to scale and transferring fourteen to cardboard (fig. 7). Dates on ten of the latter indicate Lissauer finished the sketches between May and September 1933. There is no correlation, however, between these dates and the placement of each appliqué on her quilt.

She turned to her Aunt Mildred for advice. Bagby responded, "12 x 15 . . . is a better proportion than 12 x 14. However if you have cut them 12 x 14 you could make them 11 x 14. The border should be the width of the

Fig. 8. This cloth portrait was based on an image in the July, 1930, issue of *Vogue* magazine. Kentucky Museum, WKU, 1990.6.1.

blocks."[49] She also suggested appropriate fabrics for the appliqués. "Am enclosing flesh colors that I used for face and arms & hands. No I didn't use Buty Chyne [sic] for patches as it does ravel."[50]

The "Lace-Ruffled Pantalet Days Quilt," a subscription promotion Lissauer clipped out of a 1933 issue of *The Household Magazine*, likely influenced the design of several appliqués.[51] First, one of her sketches reflects the basic silhouette and simple, large-scale print used in the magazine illustrations. Second, at least four of her figures were made from similar fabrics—solids and simple prints with the latter chiefly plaids and floral motifs. Third and finally, both projects made effective use of lace.

Lissauer was aware of a series of five articles on the history of fashion that appeared in *Vogue* between May 1929 and September 1934. She borrowed elements from drawings in the feature "1840s Costume" as source material for at least three of her figural appliqués.[52] Lissauer rendered the "lady" in winter garb most faithfully, stitching her twice before ultimately framing one version and using the other effort on her quilt (fig. 8). The application of bouillon knots on both fabric portraits suggests ermine, but from the gold buttons fastening her wrap to its green and white striped lining, the figure placed on the quilt (Row 4, #1) is noticeably more elegant.

She often combined elements from multiple sources. The spinning/knitting figure (Row 1, #1) drew upon a graphic used with the "Piece Bag" column in *Needlecraft* from 1931 through 1936 and from an illustration on a bridge score pad (fig. 9).[53] In her pencil sketch, Lissauer kept the orientation of its elements the same as depicted in both image sources, but she reversed their direction in the finished appliqué. As with ten of the other portraits, a stylized braided rug, a traditional craft item associated with the Colonial Revival, helps anchor the figure to the quilt.

Fig. 9. This illustration from *Needlecraft* partially inspired the design of the appliqué of the knitting/spinning figure (Row 1, #1).

Fig. 10. This newspaper advertisement was a source illustration for the strolling couple in Row 2. Courtesy of *The Courier-Journal.*

Details from an illustration in the "1840s Costume" article and an unsourced ad for roofing tiles were incorporated into another appliqué.[54] Lissauer kept the general stance of the figures in the fashion piece but added the pantaloons worn by the young girl in the ad and substituted its hoop for the tennis racket carried in the costume feature. Her atypical fabric choices—strong blues and reds in solids and large bold prints— may explain why she framed the completed figure rather than use it on her quilt. This "lady" was not donated to the Kentucky Museum but remains in the Lissauer family.

For an appliqué of a strolling couple (Row 2, #2), she borrowed the image of a festively dressed pair, complete with billowing muffler and lace

Fig. 11. Adapted from several design sources, this appliqué manifests the success of the collaboration between Lissauer and Rigsby.

pantaloons, from a holiday shopping advertisement for Stewarts, a Louisville area department store (fig. 10).[55] An ad for formal wear was the model for the man's cape, and a stencil-like greeting card inspired the woman's bonnet and profile orientation of both figures.[56]

An appliqué in the third row (Row 3, #2) is another example of how Lissauer employed multiple design sources—in this case, the bouquets in

Fig. 12. Lissauer adapted the illustration on this card for the appliqué on the kneeler she placed before the "Shrine to Beauty" in her home. Courtesy of Department of Library Special Collections, WKU.

an ad for bridal gowns, an illustration of southern belles clipped out of *Vogue,* and a mailer advertising a sale in Louisville.[57] The figure stands before an embroidered wrought iron fence accented with climbing vines and flowers with the visual impact of her costume heightened through the skillful application of lace, ribbons, and embroidery (fig. 11).

A magazine illustration of a woman and begging dog inspired one of the more charming appliqués (Row 2, #3). Lissauer eliminated the flowers, reversed the orientation of the figures, and chose an orange plaid fabric consistent with the color palette used elsewhere on her quilt. Decorative touches include lace mitts made from straight and couching stitches, white satin ribbons, and red-orange buttons. A note penciled on the back of its accompanying cardboard sketch indicates the plaid fabric cost twenty-two cents per yard at Sears, Roebuck.

Lissauer masterfully adapted the strolling couple from a baby congratulations card into an appliqué (fig. 12).[58] First, she eliminated the baby carriage used in the original artwork, then clothed the female figure in fabric suggestive of the garment worn in the illustration and dressed the man in more subdued attire. Next, Lissauer embroidered a wrought iron fence and climbing vines on a piece of the same sateen used for the foundation of the *Godey Quilt* and added a three-sided border of upholstery fabric. Finally, she stitched the appliqué to the sateen and covered a doorstop with the resulting textile. Lissauer used it as a "kneeler" before the "Shrine" or "Altar to Beauty" in her home.[59]

In addition to the doorstop appliqué, Lissauer made at least five others that were not used on the *Godey Quilt*. She framed three of them and converted the remaining two into pillow covers. Two of the five were slightly different and less successful versions of appliqués that were incorporated into the quilt, but the others were unique designs. Lissauer perhaps felt the latter three were unsatisfactory artistically or technically, or did not complement her overall vision.

A Touch of Embroidery

Lissauer hired a professional seamstress, Ollie Rigsby (1888–1986) of Bowling Green, Kentucky, to embellish her "ladies" with embroidery. Although Lissauer was in charge, their correspondence reveals a surprising degree of give and take in which Rigsby, a self-employed contractor who was in the subordinate position, felt comfortable in helping set the terms of her employment and in guiding her client to make good decisions regarding the form the embroidery enhancements would take.

> It took me three days to make the lady. I think I could count on making one in two days and it would be steady work, making one come to $6.00. This one I have already made is $5.00 and 15¢ for mailing. . . . I could not afford to give up my "monogram" work for less, as it keeps me busy.[60]

Lissauer had a strong sense of what her quilt should look like and was not hesitant in letting Rigsby know this. Perhaps the most useful document in their correspondence is a two-page letter outlining her directions for eight appliqués.

> Please don't mind if I am very explicit, but I have my vision of this quilt in my mind so clearly that I couldn't stand it if it didn't

Fig. 13. Lissauer used delicate embroidery enhancements to transform the appliqué modeled after this bridge tally cover into a figural portrait that reflected her vision.

turn out just that way. . . . I have tried to make it as clear as possible, but if there is anything I have left out, please call on me to straighten you out before you go ahead, as I am very anxious that they look like the vision I have been carrying around in my mind for months.[61]

Lissauer also expressed confidence in Rigsby's abilities, writing that she was "sending along a few blocks that need those artistic touches that only you can give. . . . I hope you realize that it is a great big compliment

Fig. 14: Lissauer specified the embellishments Ollie Rigsby added to the "flower box ladies" appliqués in row 5. Kentucky Museum, WKU 1990.6.1.

to you when I trust you to work on these quilt blocks over which I have labored so earnestly. I would not trust them to anybody else in the world.[62]

She was quite specific about her vision for the figure of a girl playing a piano (Row 1, #2) which was based on a bridge tally cover (fig. 13). "I have cut out the body of the piano from black broadcloth which I want you to pad with cotton and place in the right spot to fit on the legs. . . . Make it the exact size of the drawing too. I also want pink roses around her neck as illustrated in the drawing."[63] Rigsby's response, complete with stitch diagrams, was, "got your things and think I under stand [sic] then if I don't will let you know. I guess you mean flowers around the neck of dress like embroidery flowers other words [sic] Satin stitch [diagram] is it, instead of wrap stitch [diagram] like this."[64]

Lissauer sometimes sent illustrations with her instructions. For the spinning wheel appliqué (Row 1, #1) she wrote, "I am enclosing the magazine picture ... I copied so that you may see the details—how they are carried out."[65] Her notes concerning the ladies with flower boxes (Row 5, #1–#2) included an image and the following directions:

> I want you to fill in the flower boxes so that they don't look so
> bare. I am pinning a picture of a lady with a flower box behind
> her to show what I mean. . . . On the ground under the boxes, I
> want a few sprigs of flowers and grass just as many as I have indi-
> cated under the lady from *Vogue*. As you will see, one of these
> ladies already had part of the sprinkling under foot.[66] (Fig. 14.)

Their exchanges when the two women disagreed were informative. Regarding the spinning wheel, Lissauer wrote,

> On block #1 I want you to embroider the spinning wheel in black
> yarn—just exactly like the picture on cardboard. On the wheel
> part use two fine lines outside of the solid ring and two fine lines
> of black yarn inside of it. Work all parts—legs cross pieces and
> all—(except the wool in a bunch) in black. Make all this very well
> padded so that it will stand out and look rich.[67]

Rigsby responded by advising Lissauer to rethink her approach. "You said make spinning wheel in black yarn but, my dear child, it would be impossible to embroider these fine lines that close together in yarn. However I don't want to spoil your 'Vision.' Let me know."[68]

Lissauer wanted to add a signature to the *Godey Quilt*, but the two women differed over how it should look.

> Your letter came too late, however after you get your 'ladies' if you think it will not be too late, send me another piece & I will do the name over. I like the one I made better tho' because this last one would not look as hand-made. The line all around the name would look like it had been cut out & put on.[69]

Ultimately, Rigsby won this battle and did not frame the signature with a decorative linear border. The final version included the text, "Mildred Potter Lissauer/Her Quilt/1934," and one of three spools of thread depicted in Lissauer's drawing.[70]

The two women discussed the merits of the ruffle Lissauer planned for her quilt, with Rigsby maintaining that the "[border] ruffle would detract from the art of the ladies. It will be more 'artful' just quilted beautiful with-out [sic] the ruffle."[71] Lissauer initially acceded to Rigsby but saved an underskirt made of matching Buty Chine in a box of fabric remnants. She eventually won the argument as an article published in a local magazine fourteen years later indicated that the quilt was displayed on a bed with a ruffled underskirt made from a petticoat.[72]

Towards the end of the project, several letters imply Lissauer's growing impatience. Registered mail receipts indicate that she sent appliqués to Rigsby on December 29, 1933; January 6, 1934; and February 1, 1934. The exact date of the latter's response is unknown, but several letters imply it was after the first of the year. "I am so sorry I haven't written you before but I haven't had time. I have been going with my tongue out ever since before Xmas. Don't worry over your "Ladyses" [sic] for I have them & I think I can mail them to you about the first of the week."[73] Another letter documents the payment received by skilled needleworkers: Rigsby charged $5 for embroidering highlights on the spinning wheel; $2 for the piano; $1 for the two fences; $2 for the flower boxes; $2 for stitching the name; and 50 cents for the thread.[74]

Stitching It Together

Lissauer affixed the completed appliqués to six fourteen-inch-wide panels made of peach-colored Buty Chine and added an eighteen-inch-wide border of matching fabric on three sides. She likely chose this material on the recommendation of her Aunt Mildred but, possibly, she was also familiar with Ruby Short McKim's endorsement of Buty Chine as a "a permanent luster satine [sic] of finest quality" . . . "the finest materials certainly do make the loveliest quilts."[75]

When Bagby learned that her niece was having troubles getting the appliqués to lie flat, she wrote, "I am distressed to hear about the bad luck you are having with your quilt. . . . Was it the figures or the Butychynne [sic]. Be sure to bring it down and let me see it as I hear it is a gem. . . . We will discuss what can be done when you come."[76] She also recommended that her niece keep her "iron hooked up for you must press, press, press!!"[77]

Lissauer's final act was hiring someone to quilt her masterwork. This was an era when "the labor in quiltmaking was commonly divided, with one woman piecing or appliquéing the top and another woman or group of women quilting it."[78] Carrie A. Hall recommended women "turn it over to an experienced quilter, for a beautiful quilt may be made or marred by the quilting."[79] Anne Orr would arrange for a quilter who would "adapt the quilting pattern to the design of each quilt. . . . Our prices [$10 to $18] depend on the closeness of the quilting lines and elaborateness of design for the work is perfectly done on all quilts."[80]

In the 1930s, the authorship of quilts made with outside help was a non-issue. Women could purchase finished blocks and/or completed quilts in various price ranges from pattern sources such as Anne Orr, Carlie Sexton, and Marie Webster's Practical Patchwork Company. The Mary A. McElwain Quilt Shop of Walworth, Wisconsin, hired local women as well as Kentucky quilters to "cut, baste, or sew sample blocks of appliqué or piece work, quilt, and bind quilts."[81] Wealthy women ordered ready-made colonial boudoir quilts and spreads and modernized appliqué quilts from the Wilkinson Quilt Company, the Eleanor Beard Studio, and other cottage industries in the Upper South and Midwest.[82] With such ready precedents, Lissauer would have had few reservations concerning the ethics of engaging someone to complete her vision.

Lissauer considered several options before selecting a quilter. She attended Louisville's local elimination competition for the 1933 Century of Progress Contest held March 19th in the Crystal Ballroom of the Brown Hotel and compiled a list of eight quilters.[83] Seven were Kentuckians—three from Louisville, one from Pewee Valley, two from Horse Cave, and one from Hodgenville. The eighth hailed from Pekin, Indiana.

Early the following year, F. H. Eads, the Merchandise Superintendent at Sears, Roebuck & Company, Louisville, sent Lissauer a list of "quilters whose work was better than the average and whom you may wish to write to."[84] Two of the eight (Mrs. Sudie Holbert of Hodgenville, Kentucky, and Miss Clara C. Johnson of Pekin, Indiana) were on both lists. Lissauer made several additions: Miss Frances Clements (Klemenz) of Louisville, who won the Louisville competition with her *Bleeding Hearts* quilt; the A. M. Caden Shop in Lexington, whose co-owner, Margaret Rogers Caden, won the National Contest with her entry, an *Eight-Point Combination Feather Star* quilt; and the Regina Shop and Alice Lace Shop in Louisville.

By today's standards, the cost of hiring a quilter during the Colonial Revival era seems negligible. In 1915 Marie Webster wrote that the usual determining factor was the number and cost of the spools of thread required, although in some areas it could run as high as five dollars per spool.[85] Eighteen years later, Martha Woods wrote Lissauer that a local Bowling Green woman charged $1.25 a spool.[86] The next year, her journal recorded that that she had "got my 1st pink quilt back from Quilter (Mrs. Campbell) $7.00 including lining" but also noted that she paid three dollars for a "Blue nine patch quilted by a colored woman—July—1934."[87] This deflation in wages likely was a result of the hard times created by the Depression, but the race of the second quilter may also have increased the disparity.

Interestingly, Lissauer did not hire Rigsby. Quilting was perhaps outside the seamstress's normal line of work; Rigsby may have had more needlework than she could handle at that moment; or she may have earned more doing other types of fine needlework. Certainly, her embroidery work for Lissauer seemed to pay more than quilting did. She advised Lissauer to "get somebody that will keep it clean, as they go. That will be the beauty of it. If you and I & had it by ourselves we could kill the bear."[88]

Several individuals helped with the quilting. Her husband reportedly sketched the design on the foundation, and Lissauer hired three women affiliated with the Regina Shop to do the actual quilting.[89] Quilted doves (two separate designs) and bouquets (single design) alternate with the appliqués, and flowering branches enhance the border. The latticework design that covers the remainder of the quilt was carefully laid out to create oval settings for the appliqués and the quilted doves and bouquets. The stitches average 1/32 of an inch, with cording inserted between the rows, giving the quilting a three-dimensional effect. A notation indicates three women worked nine hours a day, five days a week for six months—a total of 3,240 hours.

Although there is no record of what Regina Shop President Marguerite Kleinjohn (1892–1977) charged, the materials Lissauer saved allow us to speculate as to who might have quilted her textile. The list compiled during her visit to the local Century of Progress Contest includes two women affiliated with the Regina Shop: the aforementioned Frances Klemenz and Mrs. Minerva L. (Palmer) Graham. Lissauer also added Klemenz's name to the bottom of the list provided by Sears Merchandise Superintendent Eads.

Sharing Her Vision

After the turn of the twentieth century, many Americans became interested in quiltmaking and quilting competitions.

> Not only does it serve as a stimulus to those who look forward to the fair and put into their art the very best of their ability in order that they may surpass their competitor next door, but it also serves as an inspiration to those who are denied the faculty of creating original designs, yet nevertheless take keen pleasure in the production of beautiful needlework.[90]

In the depths of the Depression, quilt exhibits and contests offered Americans outlets to channel their creative energy and provided some respite from the country's economic troubles. While batting manufacturers used these events to promote their products, department stores sponsored them as a way to drive foot traffic onsite. Several competitions in the 1920s and 1930s attracted hundreds of entries and thousands of visitors, but "the granddaddy of all quilt events in the first half of the twentieth century was undoubtedly the Century of Progress competition, sponsored by Sears, Roebuck in conjunction with Chicago's 1933 Exposition."[91] The 495 entries in the local elimination contest in Louisville were among the nearly 25,000 quilts submitted nationwide.[92]

In May 1934, Lissauer's mother suggested her daughter enter the *Godey Quilt* in a contest in Topeka. "Speaking of prizes, the Household magazine [sic] advertises a quilt show in the latter part of June and fifty dollars is given for the best quilt. . . . Would you risk sending it?"[93] Her materials provide no indication that Lissauer participated in this contest, but a letter written fourteen months later suggests it was recently entered in a competition. "I am glad you brought home the bacon with it. Surely none could have been prettier or had half so much work on it."[94] The *Godey Quilt* garnered repeated attention, including an honorable mention at the 1939 National Home Show Quilt and Coverlet Exhibition in Louisville. A local newspaper noted that it was valued at the almost unheard of figure of $5,000 and had never been exhibited without winning a prize.[95] Another article began with the headline, "Dream Designing of Highland Woman Materializes in an Exquisite Quilt."[96] In 1945 *House Beautiful* published a photograph of it; three years later the bed cover rated a mention in an article in the *Louisville Courier-Journal Magazine.* [97]

Lissauer publicly acknowledged that she had received assistance, noting, "the [quilting] designs were sketched on by my husband and then were stitched and stuffed by professional quilters."[98] There is no indication, however, that she identified the quilters by name, nor does Rigsby's contribution appear in known media reports. Still, her willingness to credit the contribution of other individuals was somewhat at odds with a general outlook that valued the act of appliquéing or piecing a quilt over the process of quilting it. Taken to its extreme, this point of view was perhaps best represented by the willingness of Margaret Rogers Caden, of Lexington, Kentucky, to enter and take credit for the quilt that won the National 1933 Century of Progress Contest, even though she had done no work on it. [99]

Conclusion

Much of the historical value of the *Godey Quilt* lies in the opportunity it affords for a case study into the mindset of its creator and her quiltmaking process: "I like to create something in the back of my head and then go to work to make it come true. That's exactly what happened with this peach-colored satin quilt. I had to dream it before it materialized into what you see."[100] Rarely do the materials that influenced the design of a quilt survive beyond its creation. Existing manuscript materials housed in Library Special Collections, WKU, help uncover the quiltmaker's upbringing and family life, as well as provide details about the quiltmaking process itself. Significantly, this documentation also encompasses the period after the quilt was crafted. Taken together, this information helps researchers understand the "how" and the "why" of the *Godey Quilt*.

Made solely for artistic and personal reasons, the *Godey Quilt* differs in many ways from most quilts crafted during the early 1930s. A figural quilt, it was based on a largely original design in an era when the marketing and commercialization of patterns and kits had reached such a level of national acceptance that originality was not as highly valued as in the past. This was certainly true for the 1933 Century of Progress Contest, whose finals featured large numbers of quilts made from kits and published patterns and which did not award any prizes to quilts that represented the competition theme. Manifesting the era's interest in America's colonial past, the quilt's appliqués were inspired by illustrations published in newspapers, magazines, and other printed materials—images that were instantly recognizable to many Americans. While there are other known examples of figural quilts from this period, relatively few of them feature images adapted so literally and so broadly from the Colonial Revival era.

With its peach-colored foundation, the *Godey Quilt* more closely resembles the upscale appliqué and whole cloth quilts produced for the cottage industries of the Upper South and Midwest than it does the vast majority of appliqué quilts that date from this period. Many of Lissauer's color choices, such as Nile green and orchid, were mainstream, and she constructed her appliqués from a mix of the solids that dominated appliqué work and the prints that piecework increasingly favored. Still, the subject matter of the appliqués and level of detail Lissauer achieved through the selective application of laces, buttons, and decorative embroidery stitches set her quilt apart.

In 1990, Lissauer donated the *Godey Quilt,* doorstop, four unused appliqués, her research materials, photographs, and the *Flower Baskets Quilt* to the Kentucky Museum, at WKU, where it remains one of this institution's most treasured acquisitions. Eight years later, Lissauer passed away at the age of 101. She was a true original, who in her unique way became a standard bearer of the Colonial Revival Movement.

Notes and References

1. Merikay Waldvogel, *Soft Covers for Hard Times: Quiltmaking & the Great Depression* (Nashville, TN: Rutledge Hill Press, 1990), xii.
2. Mary Reecy Fitzgerald, "The Development of Geometric Pictorial Patchwork," *Uncoverings 2009*, ed. Laurel Horton (Lincoln, NE: American Quilt Study Group, 2009), 139–140, 162; Merikay Waldvogel and Barbara Brackman, *Patchwork Souvenirs of the 1933 World's Fair* (Nashville, TN: Rutledge Hill Press, 1993), 22–23.
3. Thomas K. Woodard & Blanche Greenstein, *Twentieth Century Quilts, 1900 to 1950* (New York: E. P. Dutton, 1988), 90.
4. Waldvogel and Brackman, *Patchwork Souvenirs*, xvi, 42.

5. Lissauer, Mildred Wallis (Potter), 1897–1998—Collector, MSS 544, Library Special Collections, Western Kentucky University, Bowling Green, Kentucky (hereafter MSS 544).

6. *Louisville Herald-Post,* n.d., MSS 544.

7. Letter from Martha Woods Potter to Douglass Woods Potter, June 30, 1919. Lissauer, Mildred Wallis (Potter), 1897–1998—Collector, MSS 482, Library Special Collections, Western Kentucky University, Bowling Green, Kentucky (hereafter MSS 482).

8. Letter from Martha Woods Potter to Douglass Woods Potter, July 24, 1923, MSS 482.

9. Conversation with Museum Director Riley Handy recalling interview with Mildred Potter Lissauer, Kentucky Museum, August 1990.

10. Helen Lawton, "Things Aren't What They Seem," *Louisville Courier-Journal Magazine,* October 17, 1948, 14.

11. Cuesta Benberry, "The 20th Century Quilt Revival," *Quilter's Newsletter Monthly,* July/August 1989, 20.

12. Evaline Johnson and Lydia Brigham, "Priceless Heirlooms of Tomorrow," *Needlecraft—the Home Arts Magazine,* February 1934, 8.

13. W. Barksdale Maynard, "'Best, Lowliest Style!' The Early-Nineteenth-Century Rediscovery of American Colonial Architecture," *Journal of the Society of Architectural Historians,* 59, no. 3 (September 2000): 345.

14. Marilyn Casto, "Concept of Hand Production in Colonial Revival Interiors," in *Re-creating the American Past: Essays on the Colonial Revival,* ed. Richard Guy Wilson, Shaun Eyring, and Kenny Marotta (Charlottesville: University of Virginia Press, 2006), 321.

15. Jeanette Lasansky, "The Colonial Revival and Quilts 1864–1976," *Pieced by Mother: Symposium Papers,* ed. Jeanette Lasansky (Lewisburg, PA: Oral Traditions Project of the Union County Historical Society, 1988), 97; Marin F. Hanson, "Modern, Yet Anti-Modern: Two Sides of Late-Nineteenth- and Early-Twentieth Century Quiltmaking," *Uncoverings 2008,* ed. Laurel Horton (Lincoln, NE: American Quilt Study Group, 2008), 111; Karl Ann Marling, *George Washington Slept Here: Colonial Revivals and American Culture,* 1876–1986 (Cambridge, MA.: Harvard University Press, 1988), 151–53.

16. Bridget A. May, "Wearing and Inhabiting the Past: Promoting the Colonial Revival in Late-Nineteenth-and Early-Twentieth Century America" in *Performance, Fashion, and the Modern Interior: From the Victorians to Today,* ed. Fiona Fisher, Patricia Lara-Betancourt, Trevor Keeble and Brenda Martin (New York: Berg Publishers, 2011), 52.

17. Ibid.

18. Beatrice Ferrell, "Interesting Embroideries for a Colonial Bedroom," *Needlecraft,* September 1927, 8.

19. Advertisement, *Needlecraft,* July 1935, 22.

20. "Twentieth Century Patchwork Quilts," *Modern Priscilla,* August 1926, 12.

21. Sharon Fulton Pinka, "William Pinch and the Rainbow Quilt Block Company," *Uncoverings 2009,* ed. Laurel Horton (Lincoln, NE: American Quilt Study Group, 2009), 46.

22. Woodward and Greenstein, *Twentieth Century Quilts,* 5.

23. Marie D. Webster, *Quilts: Their Story and How to Make Them* (New York: Doubleday, Page & Company, 1915), 156.

24. "Colonial Quilts," *Louisville Times* Needle Art Department, 1932, 4, LSC, WKU.

25. Marilyn Goldman, "The Wilkinson Quilt Company: 'America's Original Makers of Fine Quilts,'" *Uncoverings 2002,* ed. Virginia Gunn (Lincoln, NE: American Quilt Study

Group, 2002), 147.

26. Virginia Gunn, "Quilts for Milady's Boudoir," *Uncoverings 1989,* ed. Laurel Horton (Lincoln, NE: American Quilt Study Group, 1990), 89.

27. *Wilkinson Art Quilt* (ca. 1916), Quilt Index, Record No. 5D-8A-A, 2-3, http://www.quiltindex.org/ephemerasearch.php.

28. "There is Charm in This Sextet of Quilted Cushions," *Needlecraft,* September 1929, 6, 35.

29. Nettie Spoor Hanauer, "Exquisite Quilted Gifts Easily Made for Christmas," *Needlecraft,* December 1930, 5.

30. Advertisement, *Needlecraft,* February 1931, 20.

31. Conversation with Museum Director Riley Handy recalling interview with Mildred Potter Lissauer, Kentucky Museum, August 1990.

32. Merikay Waldvogel email to author, May19, 2015; http://www.quiltindex.org/ephemerasearch.php; *Wilkinson Art Quilt,* 1921, 4, Merikay Waldvogel Collection; *Eleanor Beard Original Designs in Fine Quilting,* n.d., 14, Merikay Waldvogel Collection.

33. Waldvogel and Brackman, *Patchwork Souvenirs,* 45.

34. Gunn, "Quilts for Milady's Boudoir," 89.

35. Martha Woods Bagby, journal entry, June 1933.

36. Beverly Gordon, "Spinning Wheels, Samplers, and the Modern Priscilla: The Images and Paradoxes of Colonial Revival Needlework," *Winterthur Portfolio* 33, no. 2/3 (Summer–Autumn, 1998): 164

37. Beverly Gordon, "Costume Representations of Early America: A Gendered Portrayal, 1850–1940," *Dress,* 30 (2003): 14.

38. Ibid., 16.

39. For example, see the cover of "Colonial Quilts" *Louisville Times,* Needleart Department, 1933, LSC, WKU; *Virginia Snow Studio Catalog,* 1932, 4; cover of W.L.M. Clark, Inc., St. Louis, Missouri, *Grandmother Clark's Old Fashioned Quilt Designs,* Book 21, 1931.

40. Louisville Bedding Company, *Olde Kentucky Quilts: Their Traditions, Their Beauty, Their Place in Present Day Homes* (Louisville, KY: Louisville Bedding Company, n. d).

41. Advertisement, *Woman's World Magazine,* n.d., MSS 544.

42. Agnes Heisler Barton, "It is Easy to Make and Decorate Lamp Shades," *Needlecraft,* September 1931, 12.

43. Nancy Cary, "Delightfully Quaint Bridge-Table Ensembles," *Needlecraft,* October 1930, 9; Buty Chine is described as "Trade-marked fabric for lingerie purposes and linings, in satin weave of mercerized cotton. Width: 36," in Grace G. Denny, Fabrics; *Definitions of Fabrics, Practice Textile Tests, Classification of Fabrics,* 4th ed. (Chicago, IL: J. B. Lippincott & Co., 1936), 18.

44. Cary, "Delightfully Quaint Bridge Table Ensembles," 9.

45. Ibid.

46. "Silhouetted Ladies," *Needlecraft,* October 1931, 9, 32.

47. Advertisement, *Needlecraft,* November 1932, 2.

48. Betty J. Hagerman, *A Meeting of the Sunbonnet Children* (Baldwin City, KS: Hagerman, 1979), 37, 6; Rosalind Webster Perry and Marty Frolli, *A Joy Forever: Marie Webster's Quilt Patterns* (Santa Barbara, CA: Practical Patchwork, 1992), 24.

49. Letter from Mildred Woods Babgy to Mildred Potter Lissauer, "Dear Mildred, Your letter just arrived and I will answer your questions at once as may want a prompt reply ...,"

n.d., MSS 544.

50. Ibid.

51. Advertisement, *The Household Magazine*, 1933.

52. "1840 Costume," *Vogue*, July 19, 1930, 70–71.

53. Illustration, *Needlecraft*, September 1931, 26; ephemera item, n.d., MSS 544.

54. "1840s Costume," *Vogue*, July 19, 1930, 71; advertisement, n.d., MSS 544.

55. Advertisement, *Louisville Courier-Journal*, December 19, 1933, 5.

56. Advertisement, greeting card, n.d., MSS 544.

57. Three advertisements, n.d., and illustration, *Vogue,* n.d, MSS 544.

58. Greeting card, n.d., MSS 544.

59. Conversation with Museum Director Riley Handy recalling interview with Mildred Potter Lissauer, Kentucky Museum, August 1990.

60. Letter from Ollie Rigsby to Mildred Potter Lissauer, "It took me three days to make the lady." n.d., MSS 544.

61. Letter from Mildred Potter Lissauer to Ollie Rigsby, "Dearest Ollie, Thank you for sending along the two ladies…," n.d., MSS 544.

62. Ibid.

63. Ibid.

64. Letter from Rigsby to Lissauer, "Dear Mildred: Got your things…," n.d., MSS 544.

65. Letter from Lissauer to Rigsby, "Dearest Ollie, Thank you for sending along the two ladies …," n.d., MSS 544.

66. Illustration, *Vogue,* July 1930, 71; letter from Lissauer to Rigsby, "Dearest Ollie, Thank you for sending along the two ladies…,".

67. Letter from Lissauer to Rigsby, "Dearest Ollie, Thank you for sending along the two ladies …,"..

68. Letter from Rigsby to Lissauer, "Dear Mildred: For fear I don't exactly get your idea…," n.d., MSS 544.

69. Letter from Rigsby to Lissauer, "Dear Mildred: Your letter came too late…," n.d., MSS 544.

70. Drawing, n.d., MSS 544.

71. Letter from Rigsby to Lissauer, "Dear Mildred: Your letter came too late…," n.d., MSS 544.

72. Lawton, "Things Aren't What They Seem," ibid.

73. Letter from Rigsby to Lissauer, "Dear Mildred, I am so sorry I haven't written you before...," n.d., MSS 544.

74. Letter from Rigsby to Lissauer, "My dear Mildred: If by any chance I have failed on any part …," n.d., MSS 544.

75. Ruby Short McKim, *One Hundred and One Patchwork Patterns* (New York: Dover Publications, rev. ed., 1962), 31.

76. Letter from Bagby to Lissauer, "My dear Mildred. I intended to write you the first thing this morning…," n.d., MSS 544.

77. Letter from Mildred Bagby to Lissauer, "Dear Mildred. Your letter just recd (sic) and I will answer your questions at once…," n.d., MSS 544.

78. Waldvogel & Brackman, *Patchwork Souvenirs,* 61.

79. Rose G. Kretsinger & Carrie A. Hall, *The Romance of the Patchwork Quilt in America* (New York: Bonanza Books, 1935), 46.

80. Merikay Waldvogel, "The Marketing of Anne Orr's Quilts," *Uncoverings 1990,* ed. Laurel Horton (San Francisco, CA: American Quilt Study Group, 1991) 18–19.

81. Pat L. Nickols, "Mary A. McElwain: Quilter and Quilt Businesswoman," *Uncoverings 1991,* ed. Laurel Horton (San Francisco, CA: American Quilt Study Group, 1992), 100, 102.

82. Gunn, "Quilts for Milady's Boudoir," 83, 90.

83. List, May 1933, MSS 544.

84. Letter from Eads, F. H to Mildred Potter Lissauer, January 8, 1934, MSS 544.

85. Webster, *Quilts: Their Story,* 107, 108.

86. Letter to Mildred Potter Lissauer from Martha Woods Potter, March 15, 1933, MSS 482.

87. Martha Woods Bagby Journal entry, 1934.

88. Letter from Rigsby to Lissauer, "Dear Mildred, I would have sewed the applicae [sic] pieces down…," n.d., MSS 544.

89. *Louisville Herald-Post,* n.d. MSS 544.

90. Webster, *Quilts: Their Story,* 138.

91. Woodard and Greenstein, *Twentieth Century Quilts,* 23.

92. *Louisville Herald-Post,* May 20, 1933, Merikay Waldvogel Collection.

93. Letter from Martha Woods Potter to Mildred Potter Lissauer, May 10, 1934, MSS 482.

94. Letter from Martha Woods Potter to Mildred Potter Lissauer, October 14, 1936, MSS 482.

95. *Louisville Courier-Journal,* March 10, 1939, Section 3, 9.

96. *Louisville Herald-Post,* n.d., MSS 544.

97. "This Could Happen to You," *House Beautiful,* July 1945, 62; Helen Lawton, "Things Aren't What They Seem," 17.

98. *Louisville Herald-Post,* n.d., MSS 544.

99. Waldvogel and Brackman, *Patchwork Souvenirs,* 61.

100. *Louisville Herald-Post,* n.d., MSS 544.

Protofeminst Thought in Mid-Twentieth-Century Magazine Articles

Colleen R. Hall-Patton

Like other art forms, quilting is a microcosm of its surrounding society. Thus, quilting is a possible place to find seeds of the women's movement and active resistance to consumption. From the 1940s to the early 1970s, quilts slowly underwent a change in status in magazine articles from being understood as antiques and functional bedcoverings to being recognized as art forms worthy of exhibition at the Whitney Museum in New York City. Using content analysis of over 200 popular magazine articles in the Reader's Guide to Periodical Articles *and the* Art Index, *the paper examines how changes in views of quilting preceded and paralleled the 1960s women's movement. Though the gender component was not clearly linked to quilting until the early 1970s, quilting made the personal political by questioning cultural norms that stressed mass production of goods and the strict delineation between art, craft, and home production, as well as how the magazine articles helped women see themselves as innovative and able to claim personal authority to follow their own artistic path.*

Introduction

According to Berthold Brecht, "Art is never without consequences."[1] Every cultural text, such as an advertisement, a song, a painting, a book, or a quilt, carries multiple meanings operating at multiple levels.[2] Thus, all texts are ultimately political because popular culture is an area where collective social understandings are created.[3] From this perspective, even the creation of quilts that cause no controversy or change are political because they were created by makers following accepted norms, and thus these quilts reinforce the status quo. However, by recognizing potential resistance to the status quo through new designs, techniques, or functions, this research provides a more nuanced interpretation of the political implications of quilting. Through these new systems, we can see how women in the 1950s to the early 1970s negotiated current social assumptions of themselves and their place in the world. By subverting the conventional uses of mass production or by inventing new ones, cultural production may become an area of resistance. Following the example of Dick Hebdige's *Subculture: The Meaning of Style*, this essay examines how quilters utilized mass production to communicate difference and group identity.[4]

Another way of looking at the changes in emphasis on dominant or oppositional approaches to society can be seen by who is referenced as an authority. Authority figures or experts function as molders of public views who tend to support the status quo. The 1950s has been considered the era of the expert, when the scientific management of business was the dominant model for how American society should be organized.[5] This paper examines the changing views of quilting as an art form, the role of women, and the authority defining those views.

One effect of the second wave women's movement in the 1960s has been to question the impact of gender in areas society considered gender-free. Linda Nochlin's 1970 article "Why have there been no great women artists?" began an examination of the relationship of gender and art.[6] Art offers a particularly useful view of what is occurring in a given culture at a specific time, because it encapsulates many themes of the larger culture in a succinct manner.[7] The reevaluation of art took four distinct directions. The first was to rediscover women artists who had made major contributions to the development of Western art but were not recognized by art historians, answering Nochlin's question by showing how women had been written out of art history. A second theme examined how women were represented in art: why there were so many female nudes and so few male ones, why women were portrayed so frequently as madonnas or whores, and why women were reduced to their sexuality alone or objectified.[8] The third direction was to alter the practice of art criticism to include considerations of how gender, class, and race interacted to help or hinder women.[9] The fourth area examined how theories of art that espoused the belief that biological differences between men and women extended into cultural differences viewed women not only as biologically inferior to men, but also considered the cultural production of women to be craft, while men's work was art.[10] The research for this essay encompasses the third and fourth new areas of art criticism by looking at the changes in one art form—quilting—as portrayed in popular magazines.

Method

This research analyzed the content of approximately 200 magazine articles, advertisements, pamphlets, and books published between 1940 and 1971 that included quilting techniques in their text. Magazine articles provide a national-level perspective of how quilts were perceived at midcentury. Derived from the *Reader's Guide to Periodical Literature,* the *Art Index,* and the *Humanities and Social Science Index,* the database provided an overall view of what normal expectations were at the time, trends countering those expectations, and views of domestic art, commodification, and resources available to quilters. While the indices omit certain genres of periodicals, such as specialized needlework magazines like *Workbasket,* local farming and ranching magazines with homemaker columns, and syndicated columns in newspapers, they have the advantage of providing a consistent, accessible, and replicable index.

All articles from the following six categories were examined: bedding, counterpanes, needlework, patchwork, quilts, and sewing. Articles with titles that indicated they were not quilt-related, such as ones on bedframes or woven coverlets, were excluded. Magazine articles were included in the research if they used or referenced at least one of the three quilt methods first categorized by Marie Webster in 1915 (patchwork, appliqué, or quilting).[11] Because production method rather than product was the focus, objects that were not technically "quilts" (such as appliquéd curtains, home-quilted upholstery fabric, and patchwork skirts) were included. However, the research excluded tied comforters, embroidered summer spreads, and candlewick spreads that did not use any quilting methods, though they sometimes have been grouped under the rubric of "quilts." Also omitted were articles that only included textiles made from commercially quilted fabric, unless they alluded to traditional quilts, as with the use of preprinted fabric (cheater cloth) that looked like patchwork or appliqué.

The articles were predominantly written by experts, designers, and home furnishing editors, thus skewing the articles towards idealized and marketable representations of quilting. While the articles tended to focus on culturally valued artifacts, such as rare nineteenth-century quilts, they provided a more public perspective of quilting than one would see in specialized publications like pattern catalogs marketed to those already interested in quilting.

"Reading the quilt": Negotiations of Hegemony

Hegemony is a major concept in cultural studies used to examine how ideas, values, and beliefs in popular culture support the status quo or seek to alter it. For the purposes of this essay, articles were examined for their acceptance or rejection of hegemonic norms, defining a status quo where dominant ideologies appear permanent, natural, outside history, and beyond particular interests.[12] It describes an invisible domination subtly enforcing conformity.[13] The hegemonic view of quilting, from Marguerite Ickis'1949 book, described quilts as "utilitarian home décor" and just another method of obtaining blankets and bedspreads.[14]

This view encompassed a range of assumptions about quilting: first, it was a method women used to decorate their home. Second, quilts were not connected to any art worlds. Third, quilting's traditional "painstaking" construction methods were out of step with "modern living" and mass production. Fourth, quilts were valued as collectibles or antiques, focusing on the nostalgia of the nineteenth-century quilting bee with its associations of community, pioneer life, and creating beauty from scraps; this perspective considered contemporary quilting uninteresting. And fifth, quilting was done by women to fulfill their role as homemakers beyond home decoration by being thrifty, providing presents, and doing emotional labor. These views were used as a working definition of the status quo or hegemonic visions of quilting. People use commodities to create an identity separate from mainstream culture. An example might be using purchased bias tape to appliqué a design on purchased curtains and thus personalize a mass-produced item. Hebdige said that both the semantic/ideological and the "real"/commercial converge in commodities, even though they appear to stem from opposing value systems in most subcultures.[15] He noted how commercial exploitation rapidly overtakes creativity, originality, and symbolic protest, such as the way Sears offered "beatnik costumes" in the late 1950s. In light of this commercial push, it is still crucial to understand how quilting was described and how quilters used commodities with or against the dominant culture's expected usage.

Janice Radway contends that every form of mass culture can be seen as negative and critical of the social order, at least in a faint or implicit way, such as how folk music in the 1940s to 1960s questioned dominant culture by expressing different values or by questioning dominant ones.[16] The hegemonic view of women at the beginning of the 1960s could be defined by Betty Friedan's "feminine mystique" that saw woman only as "husband's wife, children's mother, server of physical and emotional needs of husband, children, home, and never as a person defining herself by her own action in society."[17]

Stuart Hall's classic distinction of the politics of actions and meanings places texts in one of three relations: hegemonic, negotiated, or oppositional.[18] The dominant reading refers to the culturally legitimized, taken-for-granted meaning within the social order. Negotiated meanings accept the dominant codes for restricted, situated conditions while allowing for multiple contradictions.[19] Oppositional readings aim to subvert the hegemonic meanings by exposing the ideological and political underpinnings that hide racial, class, ethnic and gender biases. By exposing the dominant code and its workings, such readings create spaces for a public voice.[20]

Every magazine article can be placed, more or less, in one of these three categories. However, for this research, because so few articles questioned the status quo at all, articles were identified as being either hegemonic or nonhegemonic. Articles were considered to take a nonhegemonic stance to quilting if they questioned its craft-versus-art status, the role of creativity, handicrafts versus mass production, or if they advocated using new technologies.

Quilts were most often seen as supporting the status quo, if reasons for quilting were considered at all. During the 1940s and 1950s, about ten percent of articles questioned hegemonic norms. In the 1960s, twenty percent took a negotiated stance and almost sixty-five percent of articles in 1970 and 1971 questioned the status quo. Post-1971 articles were omitted due to the skewing effect of the quilt revival that began at that point in time, as the ties between quilting and the second wave women's movement were consciously explored.

Magazines with pertinent articles were categorized into six types based on their primary purpose and/or market: women's, home, antique/collecting, art/museum, scholarly, and general/other. The articles themselves were classified by their primary theme as antiques, "how-to," exhibition notices, scholarly, industry, folk/ethnic art, purchase and care, and advertisements. These classifications were used to examine changes through time, to whom quilt articles were marketed, and to identify differences between magazine genres. Both the types of magazines and the themes of the articles were analyzed on a decade-by-decade basis.

Of sixty-five articles in the 1940s, six took some form of nonstandard approach, all found in antiques, collector, or art magazines. Four articles focused on antique rarities or quilts that were "tasteless, curious, but not

Table 1. Magazine types for nonhegemonic articles

	1940s	1950s	1960s	1970/71
Art	2	2	5	1
Antique/collector	4	0	0	1
General	0	1	4	6
Home	0	1	2	0
Industry	0	0	2	1
Women's	0	0	0	0
Total per decade/total articles	*6/65*	*4/46*	*13/65*	*9/14*

aesthetically pleasing."[21] They all described the rarity of individual quilts and valued them for the way they broke from conventional expectations. After the 1940s, all subsequent quilt articles in collector/antique magazines focused on spectacular, but conventional, quilts. They not only thus ceased to be a source for change by not recognizing variation, but also by showing that only conventional quilts were valued.

The other two 1940s articles reviewed the 1946 exhibition of quilts by Ethel Beam at the Bertha Schaefer Gallery in New York City. Beam's quilts were described in *ARTnews* as a "new art form" whose "... texture and choice of their contrasting patterned linings makes them genuine works of art."[22] In an almost oxymoronic statement, *Art Digest* saw them as "... sophisticated quilts conceived as pictures in modern idiom, and executed with considerable art skill," even as the writer continued to refer to them as appliquéd bedspreads.[23] The quality of design, workmanship, exhibition space, and departure from expected quilt styles forced the writers to consider Beam's quilts as art, in a way that made them the exception that proved the rule that the decorative nature of women's art meant they could never become true "art."[24]

The types of magazines and the themes of articles changed from the 1940s to the 1950s, though the percentage of nonhegemonic articles remained about the same. Four of the forty-six articles in the 1950s questioned the mainstream, scattered between art, home, and general magazines, but, unlike the 1940s, not in antique/collectors' magazines. Two offered new designs and styles for quilts to fit in the "Machine Age," defining ways for a traditional craft to be modern. Two articles saw quilts as part of the 1950s art movement of textiles as art, thus questioning the

Fig. 1. This pastel quilt by Ethel Beam was made with hand-dyed fabric and has birth-dates, lucky symbols, and hearts for each family member. From Ethel Beam, "Streamlining the Art of the Quilt," *House Beautiful,* August 1956.

assumed position of quilts as outside the world of high art. The best article to exemplify this was "Streamlining the Art of the Quilt" by Ethel Beam in *House Beautiful* magazine in 1956.[25] She advocated streamlined stitching to "speed up and simplify in the space age." Rather than "stereotyped and repetitive" patterns, she recommended "painting" in quilts using applique.[26] (fig. 1) She found freedom from the traditional restraints of "tedious stitches" by using unusual fabrics like drapery and corduroy, along with "audacious combinations" of commercial trims, and darning stitches for quilting. (fig. 2) Beam saw quilting as an "antidote to boredom, tension, too much time, neuroses, and inertia. Try it and you will find it beats sleeping pills or Arthur Godfrey every time."[27]

In the 1960s, thirteen out of sixty-five articles (twenty percent) saw quilts as challenging standard assumptions, which doubled the percentage of similar articles found in the previous twenty years. The ways in which the status quo was questioned also expanded. *Time* and *Life* magazines both published articles about at an idiosyncratic English quilter whose work was described as "mystical" *(Time)* and "visionary" *(Life).*[28] (fig. 3) Three examined how ethnic quilting traditions (Cuna molas and Hawai-

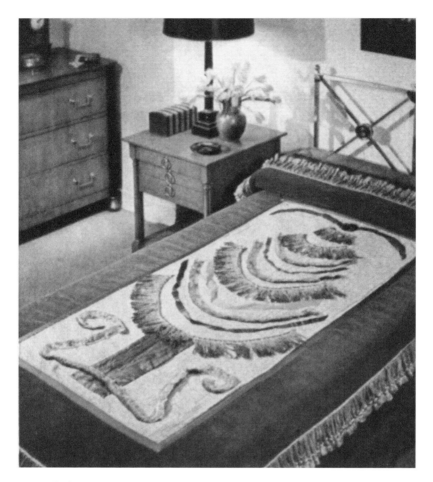

Fig. 2. The brown quilt is an interpretation of the Twelve Days of Christmas. It has a corduroy base with upholstery trim and a variety of commercial ribbons. From Ethel Beam, "Streamlining the Art of the Quilt," *House Beautiful,* August 1956.

ian quilts) fit into modern design because their abstract, yet fluid, appliqué was perceived to be more like decorative art than was the geometry of patchwork.

Four articles presented quilts as a new art medium. Two described the need for quilt design to adapt to the changed social circumstances of a new age, echoing several articles from the 1950s. The other two questioned the assumed superiority of machine-made goods, and noted that

Fig. 3. A gift of a scrap of gold fabric inspired Elizabeth Allen to create this little quilt called "Come along old queen." From "Patchwork Prophecies: Quilt Pictures of Elizabeth Allen," *Time*, June 2, 1967.

purchased goods did not provide the emotional connections to friends and family that homemade household goods offered. After the end of World War II, commercial production replaced war production and abundance replaced scarcity. While commercial production was widely celebrated in the 1950s, as it became an assumed part of everyday life in the

1960s a few writers began to question what was lost in a home saturated in manufactured goods. The articles that questioned commodity production looked at its overall impact: the industrialization of the home, the focus on product and satisfying material needs, the way producers ignored emotional needs for personal satisfaction and connecting to others through household objects, and how this left consumers adrift from their own family and national histories. As Jean Ray Laury said in *Appliqué Stitchery*,

> "We buy articles mummified in Mylar, bound in protective polyethylene and marked 'sterile.' These mass produced articles, each identical to the others of its kind, are impersonal. In many respects, they tend to make our homes identical. These manufactured items satisfy many needs: we want them, use them, and need them. But it is important to recognize what they do for us and to understand what they cannot do. We must see which needs they fill and which needs they do not satisfy. As manufactured items increasingly replace handmade articles, we lose evidence of some human involvement in our everyday environment."[29]

Five of the thirteen articles from the 1960s that challenged assumptions appeared in art magazines, four in general magazines, two in textile industry magazines, and two in home magazines. No articles questioning the status quo were published in antique/collector or women's magazines. These two magazine genres represented the most traditional viewpoints towards quilts at this point.

In 1970 and 1971, nine of fourteen articles written questioned the status quo. Three related quilts to art, three related quilts to elements of popular culture, and three noted the creation of new markets, materials and reasons for quilting. A number of these articles used a common theme first seen in the 1950s: asking whether a traditional craft technique could be relevant in a world characterized as modern and machine-driven. Some saw quilts as a way to "soften the edges" and bring a human-made factor into the machine age. Some embraced new technology and the changes they saw as necessary to blend craft techniques and mass production.[30] This blending of views of individual and mass production factored in the blurring of overall distinctions between art and craft, as both production techniques and the mediums used were questioned and expanded. "Craft" at this point was a distinction between sculpture or painting and forms like weaving, glass blowing or ceramics, all of which are now often considered within the world of high art. The textile industry strove for more "craft-like" production, while the art world incorporated industrial products into art. Art and industrial production thus moved towards each other so that "top down" and "bottom up" changes overlapped. For quilting to even be considered a craft form like ceramics or weaving was a novel interpretation at this point. Quilters were encouraged to use commercial products such as iron-on tape, purchased appliqué, and trims (many identified by brand name) to make a "homemade" object.

Looking at the types of magazines that published the quilt articles questioning the status quo offers another perspective. One art magazine, one antiques magazine, and one textile industry magazine each published one nonhegemonic quilt article, while six such articles appeared in magazines aimed at the general public. Again, no articles of this type appeared in women's magazines, or in home magazines. Other than an article in *Parents* magazine proposing new uses and novel materials for quilts, none of the articles questioning the status quo were in magazines primarily aimed at women.

The percentage of magazine articles questioning the assumptions about quilting doubled in the 1960s; by the early 1970s, they appeared at six times the levels of the 1940s and 1950s. A few articles began considering quilts as art and questioned their status as merely craft in the 1950s. Art magazines in the 1950s published the earliest articles blurring the art/craft dichotomy. Textile industry journals began to make this new association during the 1960s, and general interest magazines picked it up in the 1970s. Still, these issues were not seen as an example of the secondary status of women's art forms until 1971. Women's magazines published eleven percent of the quilt-related articles during the time period, barely more than textile industry magazines. Of these, however, not a single women's magazine published a nonhegemonic article, though three articles appeared in home magazines and one in a general magazine aimed primarily at women. This seems to substantiate Friedan's claim that magazines were a repressive force for women.[31] The more gender-neutral nature of magazines where nonhegemonic articles appeared may have generated wider acceptance for quilts bucking the status quo in art and general audiences. However, women did not find such support in magazines written for them.

There were proportionally fewer articles about quilting in women's magazines in comparison to other magazine genres, even without specifi-cally looking for questioning of the status quo. Notable exceptions were based on individual editors, such as Vera Guild at *Good Housekeeping,* Dorothy Brightbill at *American Home,* and Roxa Wright at *Woman's Day.* Individual editors were very important for championing craft forms and determining how they were presented. In contrast to women's magazines, there was support for quilting in home magazines, though quilting was usually seen only as a home decorating option. That women's magazines had the second lowest percentage of nonhegemonic quilt articles of all magazine types emphasizes again their weak support of women's art forms.[32]

Through the early 1970s, women's magazines were the most conserva-tive and slowest to adopt new views of quilting. Magazines' need to keep advertisers happy seemed to make them even more conservative than the books about quilting printed at the same time. Questioning was found in magazines aimed at the general public, the fabric trade, and art worlds (where change was an expected part of the cultural milieu), while women's magazines were the most oblivious to change.

Designers, experts, and professionalization

Articles often used some form of authority reference to support their po-sition. One way to examine hegemonic relationships is to look at who was recognized as an authority, how that authority was wielded, and how pub-lications sought to influence quilters. Authority was defined as references to experience, professional affiliation, or training. Citations such as "noted quilt expert," "museum curator," and "designed by the editors," or noting a designer's art training or profession as an art teacher, are exam-ples of these authority references. Some authority was inferred, such as references to a movie star implying class and taste. References that demonstrate artistic expertise help tie quilting to creativity and quilts to art, and present women as innovative and controlling another portion of their lives.

Daniel Bell, Marty Jezer, and Elaine May have all discussed the 1950s as the era of the expert followed by a decline in the "rebellious" 1960s.[33] While the 1950s articles do reflect the impact of institutional and commer-cial references by having magazines or editors as the most frequent type of authority referenced, the percentage of authority references is intermedi-ate between the 1940s' and the 1960s' percentages. (See table below.)

Table 2. Percentage of articles referencing authority

Decade	No. articles/total	Percent
1940s	39/65	60%
1950s	30/46	65%
1960s	45/64	70%
1970/1	12/14	86%

Table 3. Authority reference by type

	1940s	1950s	1960s	1970–71
Quilt experts	9	5	5	0
Museums/professionals	12	6	8	3
Artists/art training	1	2	7	2
Designers/decorators	8	7	12	4
Editors/magazine	8	7	5	3
Stores	1	0	0	4
Other	9	2	3	0

From the 1940s to the early 1970s, authority references in magazines became more focused into fewer categories, and their overall use increased every decade. In the 1940s, the dominant authorities were quilt experts and museums, in the 1950s magazines and designers, in the 1960s designers and artists, and in the 1970s designers and stores.

The authorities the magazine articles relied upon were categorized as quilt experts, museums or museum professionals, artists (defined by job or training), designers and decorators, a magazine authority (such as "home editors" or the Good Housekeeping Institute), stores, and a catchall "other" of references that were too few and too scattered to otherwise classify. Sometimes authority was referenced indirectly, such as the designs of an interior decorator for various Hollywood stars, where both the authority of professional decorators and the star as fashion leader were used.

In the 1940s, there was more use of multiple authorities in a single article than in the 1950s and 1960s. (In 1970–1971, the number of references actually exceeded the number of articles in some years.) For the decade as a whole, the greatest number of references was to quilt experts (twenty-nine percent), followed by museums (twenty-two percent), designers (sixteen percent), "other" (sixteen percent), and magazines (fifteen percent). Prior to and during World War II, the kinds of authority mentioned were diffuse and spread over many different types, the largest category being "other" (twenty-nine percent), followed by quilt experts (twenty-five percent) and designers (eighteen percent). The "other" category included everyone from WPA supervisors to pageant writers, to celebrities. There was a dramatic drop in this "other" category after the war. From 1946 to 1949, quilt experts and museums accounted for sixty-one percent of all references to authority, which reflected the large number of articles on museum exhibitions in those years. Florence Peto, in particular, was a major influence during this time. She was a noted writer, researcher, speaker and collector who curated a number of the mentioned exhibitions.

In the 1950s, authority use was more evenly spread between four categories, which accounted for eighty-six percent of all references. Designers and editors/magazines each accounted for twenty-four percent of the kinds of authorities cited, closely followed by museums at twenty-one percent. The fourth category was quilt experts, who comprised seventeen percent of citations. Other reference types were less than ten percent each and scattered among the remaining types. This decade showed the greatest use of magazines and editors as authorities, in comparison to being mentioned in fourteen percent of articles in the 1940s and thirteen percent of articles in the 1960s. This fact seems to reflect the emphasis on consumption that characterized the 1950s and the leading role of magazines as purveyors of taste and product availability.[34] The scientific emphasis can be seen in the use of magazine-sponsored institutes and testing laboratories. The professionalization of home decorating was seen in the increasing use of designers for creating quilt patterns and the room decor presented in illustrations. Many of the articles described how women could fulfill their roles as household manager and controller of expenses, and save money by doing their own decorator and upholstery work, rather than hiring a designer or interior decorator to help.

Unlike the historically based patterns created by quilt experts in the 1940s, designers from the 1950s forward created innovative patterns derived from their professional artistic training. Designers (professionally trained in an art-related area) were consistently the top authority from the 1950s to the 1970s. Use of this art-based expertise illustrated how quilts were increasingly referenced within an art context with reduced ties to history, providing yet more evidence of the growing consideration of quilting as art.

In the 1960s, designers and art references together constituted forty-eight percent of authority references. Designers were the most frequent authority reference with thirty percent of the total, which is higher than either the 1940s or 1950s. Designer use was one facet of the increasing art emphasis that included higher rates of both art and craft references; such use blurred the lines between high art and the decorative arts.

The second highest authority referenced in the 1960s was museums and/or museum professionals (twenty-eight percent), and the variety of venues and types of quilts mentioned grew considerably. Quilts were described as both fine and decorative art and were cited as being found in both art and history museums. Historic and contemporary quilts and artifacts made with quilting techniques were described in equal proportions. The folk art and ethnic art exhibitions discussed in the articles included both contemporary and antique quilt artifacts, as well.

In the 1960s, artists provided the third-most used source (eighteen percent) of information. Artists were less than ten percent of overall authority references for the whole 1940–1971 time period, but seventy percent of those references are in the 1960s. This increase occurred partly because magazines switched from using nameless magazine staff to identifying individual designers and artists, whose authority stemmed from their training and jobs rather than the prestige of the magazine itself. This change more closely aligned quilting with art by using named artists. It is analogous to the contrast between anonymous workers in workshops and named artists, which has been one way craft has been differentiated from art since the Renaissance.[35] Quilt experts accounted for thirteen percent of references to authority in the 1960s. Magazine editors and "institutes" also accounted for thirteen percent of authority references in the 1960s. This was nearly the same percentage as in the 1940s (fifteen) and well below the 1950s (twenty-four).

In the early 1970s, stores and designers each accounted for twenty-five percent of authority references, followed by museums (nineteen percent), magazines (nineteen percent), and artists (twelve percent). Experts and "others" disappear completely, a decline that began in the 1950s. Stores had been mentioned as an authority reference only one other time in the previous thirty years; together with magazines, stores constituted forty-four percent of authority references, demonstrating a dramatic increase in the commercialization of quilting. While the early 1970s added a different kind of corporate authority, this did not eclipse the continuation of designers and artists as authority figures, who accounted for the remaining thirty-seven percent of references.

From 1940 to 1970, seventy-five percent of magazine articles referenced some form of authority, while only fourteen percent took a non-hegemonic approach. The use of authority was part of a larger social structure of authority creation and maintenance. While designers and artists were expected to be innovative as part of their practice, overall use of their authority reinforced the status quo. This strong reliance on expertise encouraged quilters to stay within the bounds of acceptability. It made those few voices offering alternative views seem even more daring. Through time, the reduced references to authority and the increased questioning of the status quo combined to create a new context of innovation and personal authority for quilters.

Quilts and Art / Quilts as Art

From 1940 to 1970, three trends created or strengthened links between quilts and art. The first one began in the 1940s, when connections to folk art and ethnic art also made quilts more acceptable as an art medium. While Hawaiian quilting had been recognized as a separate but related form of quilting since the 1930s, the 1960s brought recognition of other ethnic applications of quilt techniques, as textile industry writers and museum exhibitions explored the designs of Cuna appliquéd blouse panels, known as *molas*.[36] This interest expanded in the 1970s to include Amish, Afghan, Indian, Tibetan, and other quilt traditions.

Second, beginning in the 1950s, textiles became an acceptable new art medium. This art connection became especially noticeable in the 1960s in articles concerning school art projects, where textiles became an approachable medium because of the familiarity of cloth. Wall hangings also became an important new kind of end product; seventy-one percent of all references to wall hangings occurred during the 1960s. Quilts as wall hangings were understood as being similar to tapestries, and thus freed from considerations of wear, usage, and washing. This allowed more focus on construction, composition, design, and color, which eventually filtered back to more traditional forms like bedcoverings.

Third, by the 1960s, quilting was less often seen as part of women's role as home decorators creating a useful product, and more as an expansion of personal expression and creativity. Quilting as a mode of personal expression in itself represented a new way of understanding women's activities. Quilts became important for the positive impact they had on how women felt about themselves for making them. Enhancing women's sense of creativity and personal identity through quiltmaking became as important as the product itself.

Still, quilts were neither consciously tied to the women's movement, nor considered a feminine art form until the early 1970s, after nearly twenty years of increasing acceptance of textiles as a fine art medium. Expanded interest in quilt techniques found in folk art, ethnic art, clothing embellishments, and wall hangings broke down traditional hierarchies of art and craft. Magazine articles cited artists and designers most frequently as authority figures, while over sixty percent of early 1970s articles took some form of oppositional stance to common assumptions about quilting. The foment of the women's movement along with all these changes were brought together in reviews of the Whitney Museum's 1971 trailblazing quilt exhibition, "Abstract Design in American Quilts." David Shapiro's exhibition review, published in *Craft Horizon,* is one of the very first essays to document how these aspects were all woven together.

> ". . . (T)he sociological imagination is stirred in shame by the thought of the stintless spirit of the women. . . . Here is a spirit in answer to Rimbaud's almost haughty call for women to be poets. They already were, as Elaine de Kooning with Rosalynn Drexler pointed out in *Art News'* "Women Issue" last year. . . . We have been irresolute too long on this "woman" question, and the deep game and cross-purposes of these quilts make the old hierarchies and rejections ridiculous. . . . we no longer must consent to the agreeable obscurity of woman-as-artist. Here is woman, in the luminous wounds of these quilts."[37]

Articles and books showed an increased emphasis on the aesthetic component of quilts and on quilts as a form of creative expression in the 1960s. Magazine articles named their pattern designers, who were often women, and emphasized their art backgrounds. The spate of articles about school art classes using appliqué for wall hangings further connected quilt techniques to the high-art concept of art as nonfunctional, while emphasizing quilts' visual similarity to paintings. The increased numbers of aesthetic references helped place quilts and quilt techniques more firmly within the sphere of art.

Quilting was progressively seen as more connected to the worlds of art-as-craft or fine art. Especially after the mid-1950s, more writers linked quilting to the movement to accept textiles as a valid high art medium. While the view of textiles as a means of personal expression and as a viable art form grew from the 1950s onwards, the gender basis of art hierarchies was not "discovered" or discussed in relation to quilts until the early 1970s. At that point, textile art—and quilts in particular—became a major part of the discussion of the secondary status of women's art forms. Notably, Patricia Mainardi asserted that a knowledge of needlework was as important to women's studies as a knowledge of African art was to black studies.[38]

Creativity, domesticity, consumption

From 1940 to 1970, magazine articles assumed that women's lives were focused on home and family. In the magazine articles, there was no return to domesticity after World War II. Women were always posited as homemakers—a focus on home was assumed as the justification for quilting. The new consumer economy after the war gave women a choice to make or buy home furnishings like quilted bedspreads and upholstery, and whether to fulfill their responsibilities for maintaining family ties, providing gifts, homemaking, and decorating by making or buying goods. After fifteen years of the Great Depression and war, magazine articles in the 1950s only saw wonder and beauty in the plethora of newly available consumer goods. Not until the 1960s did writers see and question the different values associated with home versus commercial production. Some writers also saw how the changes propelled women into the marketplace and away from creative, relaxing activities.

In the 1940s and 1950s, magazine articles emphasized women's roles as home decorators. In the 1960s, articles focused less on their roles relating to the house and to others, and instead emphasized personal expression and self-fulfilling activities. Quilting became part of this changing view of women's activities, from emphasizing the fulfillment of others' needs to realizing the importance of self-fulfillment. The magazine articles show how perceptions changed to value women as individuals with desires and needs of their own.

By seeing women's cultural production as creative beyond providing for their families' material needs, quilting gave value to women as individ-

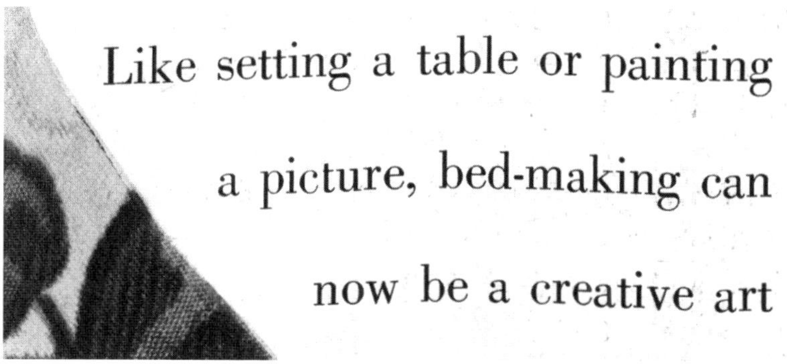

Like setting a table or painting a picture, bed-making can now be a creative art

Fig. 4. Wording in articles conflated creativity and consumption. From "Bedding isn't what it used to be," *House Beautiful*, February 1964.

uals. Using quilts to personalize their homes provided women with a way of stepping outside their expected role as the prime purchasing agent and consummate consumer and shopper for the family. In that way, women simultaneously questioned commodity culture and became producers rather than consumers.

How does an emphasis on creativity change the perception of quilts as art? Since the Renaissance, high art has focused on the creativity of the individual artist as a major determinant of the value of art. Researchers, such as Barbara Brackman and Ricky Clark, have described the 1950s and 1960s as a time of rote copying of a few standard patterns with little evidence of originality or creativity.[39] This view continued even as Friedan referenced a marketing survey from 1945 about the "growing need of American women to do creative work—the major unfulfilled need of the modern housewife."[40] The survey's purpose was to help manufacturers market to women. Magazine articles both demeaned and validated the need for creativity at the same time, attempting to substitute the practice of purchasing goods for the production of them, such as when a 1964 *House Beautiful* article stated that making a bed was "as creative and challenging as setting a table or painting a picture."[41] (fig. 4) If there was little interest in creativity, one would expect that magazine articles would show decreasing discussions of creativity—but that was not the case. The magazine articles revealed that creativity was of growing importance to quilting (though the 1940s and 1950s are nearly identical). Creativity was referenced in twenty-six percent of articles in the 1940s, twenty-eight percent of articles in the 1950s, thirty-seven percent of articles in the 1960s, and forty-four percent in 1970–1971. These numbers paralleled increases in references to the way time for quilting was seen as a means of artistic or personal expression (sixteen percent in the 1940s, twenty percent in the 1950s, twenty-eight percent in the 1960s, forty-four percent 1970–1971). Time for creativity was also accorded greater value than leisure time. In this way, writers subtly shifted the discourse on quilting by valuing process as much as product, and reimagining quilting as an area to get away from standardized patterns and design in order to be creative.

Articles by Jean Ray Laury combined art, design and quilting, consciously setting an example for her female readers of how one could bridge art and domesticity. She advocated designs that came from everyday activities and places like children's drawings and the kitchen, while using basic sewing skills and leftover fabric.[42] Quilting refuted the idea that art transcends everyday life, because so much of it was and is made for everyday living. Laury's assumption of universal creativity was a refreshing alternative to Friedan's acceptance of the heavy-handed effect of commercialization. Laury's approach countered the ideology that popular culture was only a product of capitalist commodity production with no meaning except for how it created a profit.[43] In addition, Laury included works by contemporary artists using quilts as a medium in her 1970 book, *Quilts & Coverlets: A Contemporary Approach.* As she said, "Only recently is the influence of contemporary art once again seen in our quilts."[44] Some of the quilts incorporated political statements that critiqued mass production, the status of women, and the concern for ecology, while others utilized contemporary art forms executed as quilts. Laury did not place them within the context of any social movement, but acted as an interpreter between the worlds of high art and home production, showing how women, too, could be artists using their creativity with familiar mediums.

Conclusion

Magazine articles both reflected and helped mold views. Articles that encouraged avant-garde approaches to quilts and quilting by questioning the art/craft dichotomy and proposing that textiles should be considered a valid art medium first occurred in art magazines in the 1950s. As a way of defining trends, textile industry journals like *American Fabrics* took this approach in the 1960s. Textile industry articles were directed at those who saw their role as shaping American taste and molding it to what the textile industry could provide. For them, a more artistic orientation was a potential marketing tool. Home magazines were the first type of consumer-oriented magazine to use the viewpoint of quilts as art objects; women's magazines were the very last to make this link.

One way these perceptions changed was by looking at quilting in new ways. The number of nonhegemonic quilt articles grew from ten percent of articles in the 1940s and 1950s to twenty percent of articles in the 1960s, and sixty-four percent in the early 1970s. The number of ways of questioning hegemonic norms also increased. No such articles were found in women's magazines, three in home magazines, and only one in a general magazine primarily aimed at women. Only later in the 1970s did women's magazines step away from their conservative stance that viewed quilts and quilters as part of women's sphere in the home.[45]

The 1960s laid the mental and physical groundwork for the major changes in women's lives in the 1970s. Magazine articles focused on home and family, continuing the ideal of 1950s domesticity when few women worked outside the home.[46] Changes in the 1960s were subtle in comparison to those of the 1970s. However, the 1960s differed more from the 1950s than the 1950s differed from the 1940s. In the 1960s, an early stage of the women's movement's emphasis on individuality can be seen in the use of named designers (usually women), which provided new kinds of role models for women. Writers appealed to quilters in new ways by valuing personal time and personal goals separately from women's family roles, and less often trying to justify the time women spent on creative pursuits as fulfilling wifely roles. This was part of the beginnings of a feminist consciousness as women gave themselves permission to use time for creativity and personal expression. Valuing personal needs and desires also became evident in the increased questioning of the status quo. Such views followed the path of individual transformation, one which few writers saw as common to all women, let alone tied to any broader women's movement.

Quilting was one way women expanded personal authority, increased ties to their community and increased the variety of relationships in their lives. Magazine writers presented quilts as a way to demonstrate women's creativity to themselves and encouraged women to carve out personal time and space for quilting, but they did not encourage women to change their personal situation or the larger society. That would not evolve until later in the 1970s, though articles presage this idea in the 1950s and 1960s.

Notes and References

1. Berthold Brecht, *On Theatre* (London: Methuen Press, 1978), 151.

2. Norman Denzin, *Symbolic Interactionism and Cultural Studies* (Cambridge, MA: Blackwell Publishers, 1992), 150.

3. Ibid., 137.

4. Dick Hebdige, *Subculture: The Meaning of Style* (London, UK: Methuen Press, 1979), 102. Hebdige looked at clothing and ornamentation in British youth subcultures to examine the novel and covertly oppositional uses of objects.

5. Daniel Bell, *The End of Ideology* (New York: Collier Books, 1961); Marty Jezer, *The Dark Ages: Life in the United States* 1945–1960 (Boston, MA: South End Press, 1982); Elaine Tyler May, *Homeward Bound: American Families in the Cold War Era* (New York: Basic Books, Inc., 1988).

6. Linda Nochlin, "Why Have There Been No Great Women Artists?," *ARTnews,* January1971, 22–39, 67–71.

7. William Bascom, "Creativity and Style in African Art," in Daniel P. Biebuyck, ed., *Tradition and Creativity in Tribal Art* (Berkeley, CA: University of California Press, 1969), 11.

8. John Berger, Ways of Seeing (London: Penguin Books, 1972); Rosemary Betterton, ed., *Looking On* (London: Pandora Press, 1987); Mary Bos and Jill Pack, "Porn, Law, Politics," in Betterton, *Looking On,* 182–188; Norma Broude and Mary Garrard, eds., *Feminism and Art History: Questioning the Litany* (New York: Harper and Row, 1982); Carol Duncan, "The Aesthetics of Power in Modern Erotic Art," in Arlene Raven, Cassandra Langer, Joanna Frueh, eds., *Feminist Art Criticism: an Anthology* (Ann Arbor, MI: UMI Research Press, 1988), 59–70.

9. Judith Barry and Sandy Flitterman-Lewis, "Textual Strategies: The Politics of Art-Making," in Arlene Raven, Cassandra Langer, Joanna Frueh, eds., *Feminist Art Criticism: an Anthology* (Ann Arbor, MI: UMI Research Press, 1988), 87–98; Whitney Chadwick, *Women, Art, and Society* (London: Thames and Hudson, Ltd., 1990); Rozika Parker and Griselda Pollock, *Old Mistresses: Women, Art, and Ideology* (New York: Pantheon Books, 1981); Rozika Parker, *The Subversive Stitch* (New York: Routledge, 1984); Arlene Raven, "The Last Essay on Feminist Criticism," in Arlene Raven, Cassandra Langer, Joanna Frueh, eds., *Feminist Art Criticism: an Anthology,* (Ann Arbor, MI: UMI Research Press, 1988), 227–238.

10. Alessandra Comini, "Gender or Genius? The Women Artists of German Expressionism," in Norma Broude and Mary Garrard, eds., *Feminism and Art History: Questioning the Litany* (New York: Harper and Row, 1982), 271–292; Moira Roth, "Visions and Re-Visions: Rosa Luxemburg and the Artist's Mother," in Arlene Raven, Cassandra Langer, Joanna Frueh, eds., *Feminist Art Criticism: An Anthology* (Ann Arbor, MI: UMI Research Press, 1988), 99–110; Susan Seuleiman, *Subversive Intent: Gender, Politics, and the Avant-Garde* (Cambridge, MA: Harvard University Press, 1990).

11. Marie Webster, Quilts, *Their Story, and How to Make Them,* 1915. (Reprint Santa Barbara, CA: Practical Patchwork, 1990).

12. Simon During, "Introduction" in Simon During, ed., *The Cultural Studies Reader* (New York: Routledge, 1993), 4. During's abbreviated version of Antonio Gramsci's theory reflects the current standard usage. Gramsci was an early-twentieth-century Italian theorist and politician who re-examined Karl Marx' and Friedrich Engels' writings. Gramsci's work has been subsequently refined for twenty-first-century circumstances.

13. Ibid., 5.

14. Marguerite Ickis, *The Standard Book of Quilt Making and Collecting* (New York: Dover Publications, Inc., 1949), viii.

15. Dick Hebdige, *Subculture: The Meaning of Style* (London: Methuen and Co., Ltd., 1999), 95–96.

16. Janice Radway, *Reading the Romance: Women, Patriarchy, and Popular Literature* (Chapel Hill, NC: University of North Carolina Press, 1991), 215. Radway's book examines the intersection of popular culture and gender.

17. Betty Friedan, *The Feminine Mystique* (New York: Laurel Books, 1984), xi.

18. During, "Introduction" in During, ed., *The Cultural Studies Reader,* 17.

19. Norman Denzin, *Symbolic Interactionism and Cultural Studies* (Cambridge, MA: Blackwell Publishers, 1992), 150.

20. Ibid., 151.

21. Elizabeth Marting, "Of American Quilts and Quilters," *American Collector,* Vol. 17 (March 1948), 7.

22. "Ethel Beam's Exhibition of Appliqued Bedspreads at Bertha Schaefer's," *ARTnews,* September 1946, 41.

23. "Sophisticated Quilts by Ethel Beam; Exhibition, Bertha Schaefer Gallery," *Art Digest,* September 1946, 12.

24. Parker and Pollock, *Old Mistresses,* 67.

25. Ethel Beam, "Streamlining the Art of the Quilt," *House Beautiful,* August 1956, 74–77.

26. Ibid., 77.

27. Ibid., 75.

28. "Patchwork Prophecies: Quilt Pictures of Elizabeth Allen," Time, (June 2, 1967), 53; "Art Hidden in a Bramble Patch: Patchwork Pictures of Elizabeth Allen," *Life,* August 18, 1967, 76–79. An art student discovered Elizabeth Allen in rural England, near the end of her life. Her work was described as "naïve" and "prophetic," and was compared to Grandma Moses, Paul Klee, and Picasso; it was shown in an art gallery in London in 1967.

29. Jean Ray Laury, *Appliqué Stitchery* (New York: Reinhold Publishing, 1966), 12.

30. "Impact of Blends on the Textile Industry," *American Fabrics,* Winter 1964/1965, 92.

31. Joanne Meyerowitz, *Not June Cleaver* (Philadelphia, PA: Temple University Press, 1994), 231.

32. Colleen Hall-Patton, *Quilting Between the Revivals: The Cultural Context of Quilting 1945–1970* (University of Nevada Las Vegas dissertation, 2004), 118.

33. Daniel Bell, *The End of Ideology* (New York: Collier Books, 1961); Marty Jezer, *The Dark Ages: Life in the United States 1945–1960* (Boston, MA: South End Press, 1982); May, *Homeward Bound.*

34. May, *Homeward Bound,* 157.

35. Jones in C. Kurt Dewhurst, Betty MacDowell, and Marsha MacDowell, *Artists in Aprons: Folk Art by American Women* (New York: E.P. Dutton, 1979), xiii.

36. The Cuna are an Amerindian group living on the San Blas Islands off the east coast of Panama.

37. David Shapiro, "American Quilts," *Craft Horizon,* December 1971, 42–44.

38. Patricia Mainardi, "Quilts: The Great American Art," in Norma Broude and Marry Garrard, eds., *Feminism and Art History: Questioning the Litany* (New York: Harper and Row, 1982), 331.

39. Barbara Brackman, *Clues in the Calico* (Lawrence, KS: University Press of Kansas, 1989), 3; Ricky Clark, George Knepper and Ellice Ronsheim, *Quilts in Community: Ohio's Traditions* (Nashville, TN: Rutledge Hill Press, 1991), 5.

40. Friedan, *The Feminine Mystique*, 212.

41. "Bedding Isn't What it Used to Be," *House Beautiful*, February 1964, 99.

42. Jean Ray Laury, "Be Creative with Appliqué," *Farm Journal*, May, 1966, 88.

43. John Storey, *An Introductory Guide to Cultural Theory and Popular Culture* (Athens, GA: University of Georgia Press, 1993), 14.

44. Jean Ray Laury, *Quilts and Coverlets* (New York: Van Nostrand Reinhold Co., 1970), 17.

45. Blanche Linden-Ward and Carol Hurd Green, *Changing the Future: American Women in the 1960s* (New York: Twayne Publishers, 1993), xiii.

46. Mary Ellen Zuckerman, *A History of Popular Magazines in the United States, 1792–1995* (Westport, CT: Greenwood Press, 1998), 214, 218.

Mary Catherine Lamb:
Lady of Perpetual Garage Sales

Susan A. D. Stanley

In her lifetime, Mary Catherine Lamb (1949–2009) completed nineteen quilts, most of them vivid, eccentric portraits of saints, angels, and demonic creatures. Long separated from the faith of her childhood, Lamb believed that her combination of Catholic subjects and vintage textiles and oddments both honored and affectionately skewered her devout upbringing. Scholars speculate that the "disquieting edginess" and "saucy insouciance" of her work influenced the Studio Art Quilt establishment to keep Lamb at arm's length. She never made it into that pantheon of American quilt exhibitions, Quilt National.

Using Lamb's unpublished writings, numerous newspaper and magazine articles and books, interviews of scholars and curators, family and friends, and close examinations of available quilts, this paper explores the motivations and processes behind the quiltmaker's quest to reinterpret her religious upbringing, enabling her (in her own words) to "embrace the images in a completely different way." The result is a renewed appreciation for an artist who, working almost entirely by herself (and, it is said, content to do so,) produced a unique, thought-provoking, and all-too-small body of work. At the very least, Lamb and her quilts deserve increased attention, if not a reassessment that places her as a major figure in the world of America's Studio Art quilts.

Introduction

Mary Catherine Lamb was born March 12, 1949, in Oakland, California, to Howard Lamb and Catherine Ernst Lamb. Her sister Colette was born three years later. Howard Lamb left the family in 1954, when Mary Catherine was five years old. When the girls were thirteen and sixteen, their mother married Edward Moran, an accountant who had been part of the family's life for several years. Mary Catherine is remembered by her sister as very artistic, a child who read "anything and everything."[1] She was a lifelong music fan, and her bedroom had a Beatles theme, including a group picture she created completely with charcoal dots.

The family was devoutly Roman Catholic. Like their mother, aunt, and grandmother before them, the Lamb sisters attended St. Leo the Great Catholic School in Oakland, going on to Oakland's Holy Names High School. "M.C.," as she was called, graduated in 1967, attending Merritt College in Oakland the following year.[2] In 1971, Lamb married Richard Daley, a finish carpenter, and the couple moved to Portland, Oregon, a year later. They divorced in 1978 following a two-year separation.[3]

The Quilts

Clearing out the family home in Oakland after her mother's 1986 death, Lamb discovered a treasury of carefully preserved religious objects, long-forgotten remnants of her girlhood. She was struck by the abundance of "holy cards," an important part of Catholic tradition—brightly hued, tender depictions of saints, occasionally in the gory throes of martyrdom. Long separated from the faith, she was surprised by resurgent waves of affection felt for these faded relics. "I found a lot of Catholic mementos that really stirred me," she said years later. "It was a revelation to me to realize I could embrace the images in a completely different way, on my own terms. It could incorporate playfulness and irreverence. But it also has a little bit of grief and yearning for the security of the past."[4]

Around the same time, Lamb enrolled in Marylhurst College, near Portland, chosen in part for its arrangement with the Oregon School of Arts and Crafts (OSAC), allowing the latter's students to apply craft media credits toward a fine art degree from the college. Before long, choosing wall quilts as her medium, Lamb found herself drawn to vintage linens and clothing from the mid-twentieth century, "domestic textiles from the time when I believed and found comfort in the myths and symbols of the Catholic pantheon."[5]

Early on at Marylhurst, Lamb enrolled in an art class taught by Portland art photographer Christopher Rauschenberg and multimedia artist Susan Banyas; the class explored avenues for translating life events into art. One of her first projects was *All My Hope* (fig. 1), a small wall quilt honoring her recently-deceased mother, a social worker, who had long ago abandoned youthful dreams of a singing career. Rauschenberg was immediately impressed. "I thought she was a terrific artist, thought her work

Figure 1. Mary Catherine Lamb, *All My Hope,* 1987. Measurements unknown. Collection of Colette Lamb Byington. Photograph by Christopher Rauschenberg.

was really great," he remembered.[6]

    Cootie Quilt (fig. 2) was Lamb's first quilt that really felt like it was more than following an assignment, she said. "All the fabrics in it are cut-up draperies or dishtowels or tablecloths. And I like how these cooties are funny in a way. I mean they're comical, but they also have this kind of outer-space, menacing aspect. And it also got me started on the idea of doing a series of quilts based on the shapes of old toys."[7] When Lamb quickly progressed to creating "religious" quilts, Rauschenberg became even more impressed by "the level of her craft, her vision, dealing with the religious imagery that can be traumatizing."[8]

Figure 2. Mary Catherine Lamb, *Cootie Quilt,* c. 1988. 37 x 37 inches. Collection of Renwick Gallery, gift of Nancy Becker in honor of Chris Rauschenberg and Janet Stein and in memory of Mary Catherine Lamb, 2013.81. Photograph by Christopher Rauschenberg.

The two became friends and, along with others, Rauschenberg would go to considerable lengths over the years to promote Lamb's reputation as a textile artist. He has remained her enthusiastic champion and persistent promoter into the present, years after her death in 2009.[9] Lamb's first "religious" quilt was *Our Lady of Perpetual Garage Sales* (fig. 3). As she later wrote, the Catholic ephemera unearthed in her parents' house persisted in its profound influence.

Shortly thereafter, my art history classes proceeded through Byzantine and Gothic art, imagery that I had always been at-

Figure 3. Mary Catherine Lamb, *Our Lady of Perpetual Garage Sales*, c. 1990. 35 x 35 1/2 inches. The Pacific Northwest College of Art, Center for Contemporary Art & Culture, 2010.01.01. Photo by Christopher Rauschenberg.

tracted to. It was time, in my quiltmaking seminar, to come up with a new design idea, and I thought of creating a Byzantine-like depiction of the Virgin Mary, front and symmetrical, the solemnity tempered by the unlikely combination of homely secondhand household fabrics and lush metallic. It seemed a revelation to me that I could embrace that imagery in my own way, and delight in it . . . . I didn't have to reject the beauty of the compelling, magic, historical images of the saints and angels just because I intellectually reject the dogma of the powerful institution for which these lovely images are symbols. I could approach the

Figure 4. Mary Catherine Lamb, *Saint Anthony's Torment*, 1993. 68 x 48 inches. Collection of Christopher Rauschenberg and Janet Stein. Photograph by Christopher Rauschenberg.

subjects with playfulness and irreverence in the mix, reinterpret them in my own tone. . . . And I knew I was onto something—the appropriation of historical depictions of the saints and of biblical stories, given an ironic twist with the fracturing of the overall image into slightly disjointed squares and the use of 'vintage' fabrics and splashy, if not downright sleazy, metallics.[10]

With *Our Lady of Perpetual Garage Sales,* Lamb came up with the idea of using iron-on heat transfers of photographic images, "partly as a solution to drawing (or painting or embroidering or appliquéing) a believable face, but I was so struck by the almost eerie degree of humanity it lent to the piece that I have continued to rely on this method's power."[11]

Like generations of traditional quiltmakers before her, Lamb used a familiar block construction process, but with a difference. She began with a "cartoon"—a life-size drawing of one or multiple images she wanted to include—then broke down the original composition into "essentially abstract units, unreadable by themselves," which would eventually "coalesce into the narrative only when pieced together."[12] Individual blocks completed, she would deliberately "fracture" the pieces so that they didn't fit neatly together, ultimately disjointing the images. For *Saint Anthony's Torment* (fig. 4), for example, Lamb gave a few squares a quarter-turn before attaching them to the neighboring squares. A few other squares were completely transposed, their positions swapped. The process helped "to exaggerate the kinetic sense of these 'moving pictures,'" the artist's deliberate disjunctions of the pattern alignment "introduc[ing] both motion and the notion of deconstruction of the subject."[13]

"I'm interested in the composition of each individual square, in addition to the way it's a part of this whole. That's one reason I like this kind of fracturing effect," Lamb said. "It's just a way of emphasizing their individuality, by having them not match up."[14] Certainly, the fracturing served to emphasize the theme of the original image. In the case of *Saint Anthony's Torment,* the viewer sees "an individual struggling to maintain his concentration in the face of diabolical distraction, clinging to faith and sanity while everything is spinning apart."[15] In this quilt, the body of a pig—menacing? protective?—(seen bottom left) was cut from a child's pink polka dot corduroy jumper.

Lamb's choice of textiles was anything but random, as she wrote in 1992, describing the creation of *Guadalupe Reperceived* (fig. 5), her OSAC thesis project.

Figure 5. Mary Catherine Lamb, *Guadalupe Reperceived,* 1992. 102 x 76 inches. International Quilt Study Center & Museum, 2006.043.0003

I looked through my collection of holy cards, through books of lives of the saints, coffee-table books on Russian icon painting, etc. When I came across a picture of Our Lady of Guadalupe, I recognized my thesis image immediately. I was thrilled at the potential for translation into fabric of the visual elements I saw represented—the full-body aura of spiky rays, the graceful crescent moon, the ample mantle replete with folds, the angel at her feet. . . . When I found a small tablecloth at the Goodwill with a '50s golf theme I was thrilled . . . I continued to plow through second-hand stores and garage sales in search of textiles that were reminiscent of the time. But I didn't want all the material in the piece to be of the same ilk; I wanted to incorporate some fancy metallic or brocades that would suggest the tradition of ornate medieval illuminations, of gold-leaf paintings, and I found a narrowly striped gold-and-black fabric (in the form of a skirt) that struck the right note for the rays of light beaming around the figure of the Virgin. This process of creating relationships gleaned from many sources, salvaged on their way out of one family's life and into a creative piece, is an important one. . . . Some of the other sources of fabrics include a nubbly, old-ladyish cotton housedress (that smelled like perspiration when I ironed it), curtains with a zany, architectural theme, $22 a yard peacock blue gauzy Indian cotton with metallic gold thread woven into it, rayon pajamas that I bought used long ago (and frequently wore myself) depicting stereotypical 'Chinamen' carrying parasols in a mountainous landscape, several coarsely-woven Guatemalan cottons in deep reds (I cut up one of my own skirts, worn daily on a trip ten years ago when I walked all over Manhattan), a lightweight red brocade with a pattern of roses. . . . Over 25 different fabrics are incorporated into this piece, and each selection was a separate, deliberate decision, often not easily made. Frequently when one fabric would feel right for one shape, it would preclude an earlier choice, which might affect yet another earlier-made choice. I often spent an entire afternoon pinning up many possibilities, realizing none of them were right and being unable to proceed without more forays into the land of raw material.[16]

On Portland's Southeast McLaughlin Boulevard, housed in the cavernous, long-shut Pendleton Wool factory, Goodwill's As-Is outlet store was a favorite haunt. Emerging triumphant from its odiferous, poorly-lit depths, Lamb almost invariably carried away rare gems, castoffs sold for fifty-nine cents a pound. Mid-twentieth century draperies, glittery mother-of-the-bride dresses, trinkets and luncheon tablecloths galore—all this cultural detritus emitted powerful whiffs for Lamb, relentlessly reinforcing memo-

Figure 6. Mary Catherine Lamb, *Angel at the Tomb,* 1994 or 1995. 57 x 37 1/2 inches. International Quilt Study Center & Museum, 2016.026.0001.

ries of her Catholic childhood. Among the silks, satins, brocades and metallics she gathered were "some hideous things I'd rather be shot in the foot than actually wear."[17]

Most of Lamb's nineteen completed quilts have religious themes, which can be roughly categorized into groups. Those that might be described as "somewhat beatific" include *Our Lady of Perpetual Garage Sales; Guadalupe Reperceived; Angel at the Tomb* (fig. 6); and *The Archangel Michael Bids You Aloha* (fig. 7). Lamb's version of *The Archangel Michael* bears more than a family resemblance to a vintage holy card (fig. 8). Most holy cards of the archangel depict him in fiercely glowering side view, slashing away at some fantastical demonic creature of one sort or another.

A second group, modeled after what Lamb called "medieval images including reference to hell, references that are deliberately almost comic," included *Saint Anthony's Torment* (fig. 4); *Four Horsemen of the Apocalypse* (fig. 9); and *The Whore of Babylon* (fig. 10).[18] In the particularly vivid *Saint Anthony's Torment,* the stoic saint is shown walking on flames, "enduring the provocations of four fang-baring, cudgel-wielding demons of polka-dot corduroy and pinwheel prints," she wrote.[19] Lamb also incorporated into this quilt pieces of an Asian-themed, screen-printed bridge cloth, the border of a kitchen tablecloth, 1940s barkcloth draperies and a cotton print from an unused bolt from the 1930s. As with most of her quilts, it was heavily embellished with machine and hand quilting stitches. Other quilts would find themselves festooned with bits and bobs as disparate as seashells from a necklace, buttons, sequins, fake pearls, old coins, bugle beads, and subway tokens.

Venturing into "the enchanting world of medieval monsters" provided rich subject matter. Two years later, Lamb had finished *The Four Horsemen of the Apocalypse,* complete with a skeletal rider and a gaping, flame-belching "hellmouth." *The Whore of Babylon,* also from the Book of Revelations, rides a seven-headed beast with ten horns. "I enjoy emphasizing the amusingly absurd of these medieval demons over their original menacing quality," she wrote.[20]

Her fondness for medieval demons unabated, Lamb began contemplating a project creating small "portraits" of particular evil creatures lurking in medieval sources. "They often are so wildly fanciful, with comically bulging eyes and forked tails, spreading talons and crusty scales, wicked horns and beaks and hooves that would be delightful to translate with garish brocades and 'vintage' prints," she wrote.[21] By the conclusion of the following year, 1998, Lamb had created a small bestiary of three demons:

Figure 7. Mary Catherine Lamb, *The Archangel Michael Bids You Aloha*, 1991. Silk, brocade, cotton, beads, plastic ribbon, and transit tokens. 55 1/4 x 38 1/2 inches. Portland Art Museum, Portland, Oregon. Gift of Nancy Becker, 2011.81. Photograph by Christopher Rauschenberg.

Figure 8. Vintage holy card, possible model for *The Archangel Michael Bids You Aloha.* Author's collection.

Figure 9. Mary Catherine Lamb, *The Four Horsemen of the Apocalypse,* 1995. 80 x 60 inches. International Quilt Study Center & Museum, 2006.043.00042

Figure 10. Mary Catherine Lamb, *The Whore of Babylon*, 1997. 100 x 82 inches. International Quilt Study Center & Museum, 2006.043.0005

Winged Cheetah, Scaley [sic] Beast, and *Spotted Beast.* And small they are. *Spotted Beast,* the largest of Lamb's trio of "portraits," measures less than thirty inches in either dimension (fig. 11).

She drew particular inspiration from *The Book of Kells,* an illuminated Gospel book created circa 800 AD, whose illustrations embellished traditional Christian iconography with ornate, swirling motifs.[22] Dazzled by the intense artistry of these medieval depictions of the saints, she realized that the flat, graphic quality of the illuminated manuscripts made them well suited for reinterpretation with two-dimensional textile work.[23] From *The Book of Kells,* she selected a single page depicting all four Evangelists (fig. 12), and over a four-year period she translated the quartet of images into four large quilts: *John the Eagle* (1999); *Mark the Lion* (2000);

Figure 11. Mary Catherine Lamb, *Spotted Beast,* 1998. 29 x 28 inches. International Quilt Study Center & Museum, 2006.043.0008

Luke the Ox (2001); and *Matthew the Man* (2002). While the quilts' designs were literally based on the Evangelists' portrayals as animals in *The Book of Kells,* Lamb gave them a unique flair. Her *John the Eagle* (fig.13), for example, has a background made from, among other fabrics, a souvenir tablecloth from the 1939 San Francisco World's Fair. In the background for *Mark the Lion* (fig.14), pieces cut from a cotton circle skirt screen-printed with gold ferns cohabit with hot-pink upholstery fabric, as well as an old chiffon scarf.

Not part of Lamb's *Book of Kells*-inspired quartet, *The Archangel Michael Bids You Aloha* has a background made from a vintage souvenir tablecloth from Hawaii. An old pair of nylon pajamas figures in the background of *The Whore of Babylon*. A close look at *The Four Horsemen of*

Figure 12. Folio 27v from *The Book of Kells*. Trinity College Library, Dublin. Reproduced with permission.

the Apocalypse reveals images of tiny surfers and shark fins, originally part of a Hawaiian muumuu. Given the often-witty juxtaposition of the wildly-varying fabrics, one might ask if there was a deliberate and sincere component of spirituality in Lamb's quilts. The question is fair, one to which she gave much thought.

Figure 13. Mary Catherine Lamb, *John the Eagle,* 1999. 53 x 34 inches. International Quilt Study Center & Museum, 2010.009.0004.

Figure 14. Mary Catherine Lamb, *Mark the Lion*, 2000. 53 x 33 inches. International Quilt Study Center & Museum, 2010.009.0003.

[I]n fact whatever spirituality is present in the work resides not so much in the narrative or historical element but in the process and the use of materials .... In thinking about my intense attraction to using clothes previously worn by anonymous others, I have come to realize that I feel, when handling these clothes that are infused with lived but unknowable, human experience, a profound sense of wonderment that is not unlike the awe that comes over me at the decorated grave sites of strangers at cemeteries I've visited on my travels. ... As I cut up discarded garments, I give them new life not only by reusing them individually but by conflating them into an object—a quilt—whose integrity largely depends on the success of their visual relationship to one another. The lively graphic interaction of these carefully placed fragments animates them anew.[24]

Lamb's quilts almost demand urgent emotional connection—often a sharp, heartfelt recognition of the range of emotional experience once played out in the presence of the castoffs, hinting at unknown lives, "the ordinary ... infused with the numinous," she said.[25] As with any good art, a Lamb quilt's "meaning" could be wildly different, depending on its viewer's personal history. The religious imagery might dredge up memories horrible or pleasant, perhaps within the same moment, within the same person.

With time, Lamb's quilts would be hailed as "unique, fastidious, precise, and eccentric," as was their maker.[26] "Her repurposing of Christian imagery from her youth, her use of fractured blocks to emphasize imagery, and her recycling of everyday fabrics from the 1950s, from children's pjs to tablecloths ... all her own ideas. She combined them to create a small but utterly distinctive body of work," wrote quilt scholar and historian Robert Shaw.[27]

Studying quiltmaking at the Oregon School of Arts and Crafts, Lamb was aware of America's Studio Art Quilt movement that had emerged in the mid-1960's. As did several better-known art quiltmakers unknown to her, she "worked with pictorial images and approached design wholistically, as a painter would," wrote Robert Shaw.[28] But her artistic development was independent, following her own timeline. Those who knew her and her work were impressed by the originality of her vision, recognizing the absence of obvious outside influences.

Michael James, pioneering quilt artist and author (now chair of the

University of Nebraska-Lincoln's Department of Textiles, Merchandising and Fashion Design), was one who became intrigued by Lamb's yearning for long-lost faith intertwined with vintage textiles "whispering" about their earlier lives. He wrote about the quiltmaker, shared a nearly 20-year correspondence with her, and calls her work "totally original," a product of her "quirky sensibility."[29] Others agree. "She was very much alone and happy to be, so far as I could tell," remembers Shaw. "Michael's [James's] support was very important to her, as was mine, but she was very sure of what she was doing and not really connected to the 'quilt world.'"[30] Shaw met Lamb early on, featured two of her quilts in his influential 1997 book, *The Art Quilt,* and is credited for "really put[ting] her on the map."[31]

Intrigued by Lamb's coexisting senses of whimsy and spirituality, still more quilt scholars eventually celebrated her quilts in art journals, as did many regional publications, both during her life and posthumously.[32] During her lifetime, however, Mary Catherine Lamb was not as respected in the highly competitive "art quilt" or "studio quilt" world as her supporters thought she deserved. "She was not that well-known . . . [she was] on the fringes of the quilt world, more on the periphery," James said.[33] She was seldom invited to display her quilts in prestigious exhibitions, including Quilt National, for reasons that may have varied. For one, the "saucy insouciance" expressed by her chosen fabrics, combined with the "disquieting edginess" of the fractured block construction, may have worked against critical acceptance.[34] Further, the religious content, however ambivalent, might have inspired negativity on the secular prejudices of juries.

Exhibitions and Recognition

Lamb was a member of Portland's Blackfish Gallery, the country's longest-running cooperative gallery, from 1993 through 1998, and was subsequently invited to join Nine Gallery, co-founded by nine artists, including Rauschenberg. With Lamb's four evangelist quilts completed, Nine Gallery hosted her one-woman show, "From the Scriptoria: Quilts Inspired by *The Book of Kells.*"[35] Over the years, her quilts were displayed in both galleries, in solo shows as well as in exhibitions with fellow member artists.

During her lifetime, through the efforts of her supporters—and often through her own efforts—her vibrant quilts were exhibited around the world. The résumé she created and maintained for herself lists under "Selected Exhibitions" a dozen shows of her work. Many of the exhibitions she listed were regional and elsewhere on the West Coast. But Lamb's remarkable quilts were seen in galleries and museums of other American cities: Pittsburgh, Atlanta, New Orleans, Oberlin, Ohio, and Gatlinburg, Tennessee. They were also displayed in Strasbourg, France, in Quilt Expo VI, an exhibition curated by her longtime supporter, Robert Shaw, and in the Czech Republic, with works by fellow members of Portland's Blackfish Gallery.[36] From 1999–2001, her *Angel at the Tomb* hung in the Ashgabat residence of the American Ambassador to Turkmenistan, part of the U.S. State Department Art in the Embassies cultural exchange program.[37]

Presiding over the city's lush Park Blocks, the Portland Art Museum, founded in 1892, is the oldest art museum on the West Coast. Within the museum's holdings is Lamb's *Michael the Archangel Bids You Aloha.* Bonnie Laing-Malcolmson, the Arlene and Harold Schnitzer Curator of Northwest Art, emphasizes that emerging artists—particularly female—are increasingly valued at the museum. "We like to represent artists who are doing powerful work, who might otherwise be underrepresented," she says. "Many women who work with non-traditional fine arts forms haven't really been added to our collection. Northwest women artists who have a history of good work just have not been included—because they are women." Lamb's work, she adds, was "interesting, valuable, exceptionally strong." The fact that *Michael the Archangel Bids You Aloha,* as do most of her quilts, "has an ecclesiastical bent" only adds to its appeal, she believes.[38]

For six years, *Our Lady of Perpetual Garage Sales* was appreciated for its artistry and humor at The Museum of Contemporary Craft. Earlier this year, that museum closed its doors and the quilt is now in the collection of the Pacific Northwest College of Art's Center for Contemporary Art and Culture. "It's interesting because it's a different take on what a quilt could potentially be," says Nicole Nathan, erstwhile Curator of Collections at the Museum of Contemporary Craft. "Interesting that it's figurative, and that she's really taking some topics and using them a little cheekily. She doesn't take that so seriously, and it's represented in a quilt." And there is the local appeal: "It's a nice example of a local person who's using fabric in an interesting art form."[39]

The International Quilt Study Center (now the International Quilt Study Center & Museum, or IQSC&M) was established in June 1997, when native Nebraskans Ardis and Robert James donated nearly 1,000 quilts and an endowment to the University of Nebraska-Lincoln. In 2006, Ardis and Robert James donated six Mary Catherine Lamb quilts to the Center, which would eventually own fourteen of her quilts through donation from others, or direct purchase. Carolyn Ducey, Curator of Collections at the IQSC&M, is particularly fond of the fourteen Lamb quilts. "On first viewing her quilts, you think, 'There's something *off* about her,'" says Ducey.[40] "Then you see it's deliberate, unique." Lamb's humor "has a way of leavening the dark seriousness," Ducey says. "Catholic stuff gets awfully self-important sometimes—that Catholic guilt." But there's more: "It's her sense of humor. She appreciates her upbringing, but she kind of skewers her Catholicism a little bit." "I love her technique," says the curator, "the block format, the way she breaks the forms apart, then puts them back together is really masterful." Ducey appreciates the whole package: "It's her combination of innovative artistry, and her sense of humor, and the unique, unusual way she pulls together these unusual fabrics that makes her so important to us. Just the fractured way she puts it all together."

The question then arises, why wasn't Lamb better-known and respected during her lifetime? "A lot of people knew her work and respected it, but it didn't take off the way it should have. Hard to say why," Ducey offers. As sometimes happens, this may be connected to an artist's interest in marketing her work. "Lamb was not concerned with that. She was more wrapped up in doing the work. The artistic sensibility."[41]

Eight years after her death, where does the eccentric Mary Catherine Lamb fit in the Studio Quilt world? "At the top," says Michael James, ever her champion. "She was one of the originals, in a class with people like Terrie Mangat, Susan Shie . . . [she made] things that have a more narrative line. She just took this form that had all these givens, and said, 'I'm going to throw out all these parameters.'"[42]

In November of 2009, a scant four months after Lamb's death, the IQSC&M opened a months-long exhibition called "Perspectives: Art, Craft, Design and the Studio Quilt." Co-curated by Michael James and fellow fiber artist and art critic Sandra Sider, it featured twenty-one contemporary artists whose works were in the museum's permanent collection. Lamb's *Sock Monkey Jamboree* (fig. 15) was included, keeping company with Studio Art Quilt luminaries including Terrie Hancock Mangat and Susan Shie, along with Faith Ringgold, Pauline Burbidge, Therese May and others.

Personal Life and Community Activism

Mary Catherine Lamb's quilts were made over a period spanning barely

Figure 15. Mary Catherine Lamb, *Sock Monkey Jamboree*, 2007. 64 x 45 inches. International Quilt Study Center & Museum, 2007.043.0001.

two decades, during which time she was involved in other activities vitally interesting to her. Arriving in Portland in 1972, she found the city to be sympathetic to the unconventional, a politically liberal mecca for artists and writers. Almost immediately, she attracted friends, who in later years would call themselves "M.C.'s Tribe." She loved to entertain, hosting "hard-core" monthly poker games in her home, admission requiring the ability "to contribute to discussions of life, culture and current events." She gathered her women friends, fellow "movie fanatics," for semi-monthly movie outings. The rules: no popcorn during the film, no standing up until the credits were through.[43] "M.C.'s" wide-ranging enthusiasms, including her "abiding love of music, especially honky-tonk and rockabilly," quickly made her a popular fixture in Portland's counterculture scene, as her obituary would note.[44] For all her unconventionality, Lamb could be surprisingly prim and old-fashioned. She insisted on "proper" English, and was meticulous in writing thank-you notes for favors received. Her signature "look" included a short bob with bangs, large round glasses and quirky, colorful combinations of vintage clothes—outfits that happened to tickle her fancy.[45]

As is so often true for the artistically creative, Lamb's income was erratic, deriving from an ever-changing patchwork of part-time jobs. She was night-shift dishwasher at a restaurant, clerk at the Multnomah County Library, copy editor for Pacific Northwest publishers (including *Glimmer Train, Left Bank,* Eighth Mountain Press, *Mississippi Mud,* and eventually for *Willamette Week,* the city's alternative newspaper). She also wrote and edited for technical firms. She had a successful eBay store dubbed "A Prize Every Time," peddling some of the vintage clothing harvested from her ventures into Portland's many thrift stores and garage sales.[46]

Off work, Lamb threw herself into a variety of liberal causes. Volunteering for community radio station KBOO-FM led to hosting "Women Reading Women," a semi-monthly program spotlighting fiction written by women (fig. 16).[47] In the spirit of her Bay Area youth, when she vigorously protested against the Vietnam War, she actively promoted a variety of progressive causes. While at the library, she helped organize its first union. Along with many others, she vigorously opposed 1992's Ballot Measure 9, an anti-gay measure on the Oregon ballot. Five years later, she joined OPB Watch, a committee opposing the elimination of most of the music programming on Oregon Public Broadcasting. In 2002, she organized a letter-writing campaign protesting the closing of the 127-year-old postal station in Portland's Pioneer Courthouse.[48]

An inheritance from her mother's 1986 death changed Lamb's life in several ways. While not wealthy, she became more financially secure. She left her library job, while continuing the copy editing. Still studying quilt-

Figure 16. Mary Catherine Lamb at KBOO-FM, Portland. Photographer unknown.

making at the Oregon School of Arts and Crafts, she was able to focus more on her art studies at Marylhurst. She received a Bachelor of Fine Arts degree from Marylhurst in 1992.

The Buckman House

Even as Lamb became recognized for her idiosyncratic quilts, she was nearly as well known for her eccentric home. The inheritance allowed the purchase of a century-old, ten-room, three-story house in Southeast Portland's Buckman neighborhood. With that, she could showcase her impressive, ever-expanding collection of cultural miscellanea. It quickly became an "amazing house . . . a very personal museum of things she loved."[49]

Itself a work of art, the Buckman house offered visitors a whimsical, arresting array of wide-ranging collections, each piece placed in a way Lamb found meaningful. An extended family of sock monkeys lined the window seat of her bedroom. The bathroom walls displayed assorted paint-by-number pictures. Bright cotton handkerchiefs were pinned high on a wall, like colorful little flags. Women's gloves, no two alike, served as a valance across the bedroom window. Chinese checkerboards covered one wall.[50] A small, serene figure of The Virgin of Guadalupe presided over the living room, guarded by a ring of plastic cootie toys. Elsewhere, other religious statuettes, holy cards, paintings and prayer books were arranged in abundance, a collection that, like her quilts, both honored and affectionately skewered her Catholic upbringing. Spread throughout the house were many vignettes, seemingly disparate objects juxtaposed, underscoring both their uniqueness and common spirit. Her quilts were often displayed on the walls.

Lamb regarded her collecting and quiltmaking as complementary enterprises, conveying her message with seemingly-contradictory items, like the curious juxtaposition of the Virgin Mary and her phalanx of cooties. "It's very poignant to me to see this evidence of these previous lives that these second-hand objects have," she said. "They were important to someone, they were handled, they were present for occasions. What I do with these quilts, and what I do arranging these vignettes throughout the house, there's a real similarity in the process in creating a visual whole from these things that came from far and wide. They do have that in common."[51]

The third floor of Lamb's house served as her well-organized studio, shelves and drawers crammed full with her hundreds of pieces of vintage fabric and other oddments, raw material for the quilts she pieced together and appliquéd with a vintage Singer sewing machine.[52] On the steps leading up from the sidewalk, painted wooden crutches served as balustrades, and brightly-hued bowling balls defined the periphery of the front porch. Lavishly-illustrated articles about the house appeared in regional newspapers, and at least one national magazine.[53]

Death

When Lamb was first diagnosed with breast cancer in 2004, The Tribe gathered around her, bringing food and company to her house. Five years later, as plans were being made to celebrate the cancer's official remission, it returned with a vengeance, this time attacking her liver and brain. The Tribe, now eighty-plus strong, again rose to the occasion, raising funds for her care, taking turns providing meals, and providing companionship.

She died at age sixty, on August 15, 2009, her sister Colette having nursed her through her last days.[54] At the end, she was rushing to complete a commission for her friend Christopher Rauschenberg: a mourning quilt commemorating his father, the artist Robert Rauschenberg, who had died the previous year. Her October memorial service, held in Portland's Tiffany Center, was attended by "a couple of hundred" of her friends.[55]

After Lamb's death, preserving the Buckman house was not possible. Rauschenberg took detailed photographs documenting each of the many rooms. Along with Susan Seubert's photos for *Budget Living,* they were published in a book called *Mary Catherine Lamb's House.*[56] The hundreds of items the artist had so meticulously amassed and arranged throughout her home were distributed among The Tribe.

Conclusion

Today, Lamb's reputation as an important and original quilt artist is secured, and she is increasingly recognized in national quilt communities. Her whimsical *Cootie Quilt* is in Washington, D.C., part of the permanent collection of the Renwick Gallery, home of the Smithsonian National Museum of American Art's craft and decorative art program. Fourteen of her nineteen completed quilts are now in the collection of the International Quilt Study Center & Museum in Lincoln, Nebraska. *Our Lady of Perpetual Garage Sales* resides in Pacific Northwest College of Art. *The Archangel Michael Bids You Aloha* is in the collection of the Portland Art Museum. *Saint Anthony's Torment* belongs to Lamb's longtime friend and mentor, Christopher Rauschenberg.

In September 2015, an exhibition called "Medieval Imagery in the Quilts of Mary Catherine Lamb" was held in conjunction with the University of Nebraska-Lincoln's conference, "The Material Culture of the Middle Ages and Renaissance." Curated by Jonathan Gregory, and displayed at the IQSC&M, it was the Quilt House debut of Lamb's four quilts based on *The Book of Kells* imagery.

It is likely that in the years to come, Mary Catherine Lamb's reputation as a Studio Art quiltmaker will continue to grow. Despite a decades-long rejection of Catholicism's dogma, she devised an artful, arresting way to celebrate the "compelling, magic, historical images" of saints, angels and demons. Mixing in her own brand of "playfulness and irreverence," she succeeded in de-clawing the monstrous demons feared in her youth, inviting them out to play.

Notes and References

1. Colette Lamb Byington, telephone interview by the author, October 20, 2013.

2. Ibid.

3. Daley v. Lamb (Circuit Court of the State of Oregon 30 January 1978).

4. Oregon Public Television, *Oregon Art Beat*, "Quilter Mary Catherine Lamb," Episode #105, broadcast May 5, 2000. http://www.opb.org/television/programs/artbeat/episodes/105/

5. Robert Shaw, *The Art Quilt* (New York: Hugh Lauter Levin Associates, 1997), 21.

6. Christopher Rauschenberg, interview by the author, October 7, 2013.

7. Oregon Public Television, "Quilter Mary Catherine Lamb."

8. Rauschenberg interview.

9. It is unlikely that Lamb's work would have received the attention it did without the early, consistent encouragement provided by her teacher. Christopher Rauschenberg was the only child of pioneering American artist Robert Rauschenberg who, along with fellow artist Jasper Johns, is perhaps best known for paving the way for pop art in the 1960s. A Portland-based art photographer who co-founded two of the city's art galleries, the younger Rauschenberg has edited around sixty art and photography publications, and co-curated and co-produced hundreds of solo and group exhibitions, including those featuring the quilts of Mary Catherine Lamb.

10. Unpublished artist's statement, March 1997. Held by Mary Orr, designated heir of Mary Catherine Lamb's papers.

11. Unpublished artist's thesis report, February 11, 1992, Mary Orr Collection.

12. Michael James, "Mary Catherine Lamb: Quilts Sacred and Profane," *Art/Quilt* #9 (1998), 14.

13. Ibid.

14. Oregon Public Television, "Quilter Mary Catherine Lamb."

15. Shaw, *The Art Quilt,* 235.

16. Unpublished artist's thesis report.

17. Oregon Public Television, "Quilter Mary Catherine Lamb."

18. Unpublished artist's statement.

19. Ibid.

20. Ibid.

21. Ibid.

22. *The Book of Kells,* widely regarded as the most beautiful illuminated manuscript surviving from the early Middle Ages, is believed to have been created circa 800 AD in a monastery in either Britain or Ireland. A masterwork of Western calligraphy and illumination, the manuscript exemplifies Insular style, produced from the late sixth through the early ninth centuries in Ireland, Scotland and England, as well as in continental monasteries. Calligraphed in ornate script, the book contains the Latin text of the four Gospels of the Christian scriptures, accompanied by many full-page miniatures. A multitude of smaller painted decorations appear throughout. The illustrations were done in a broad range of colors: purple, lilac, red, pink, green and yellow being most often used. Centuries after its creation, following a tumultuous—often disastrous—history, ranging from Viking raids to ill-conceived (if well-meaning) "restorations," the book is now housed in the library of Trinity College Library, Dublin. It is deemed Ireland's finest cultural treasure.

Four of Lamb's quilts, completed between 1998 and 2001, were based on a depiction of the four evangelists from Folio 27v in *The Book of Kells*. While meticulously replicating the images themselves, Lamb again blended whimsy with nostalgia for her long-lost faith, selecting from her stash a variety of mid-twentieth century fabrics: bits of clothing including a chiffon scarf, a souvenir tablecloth from Hawaii, and upholstery material among them. Lamb's four evangelist quilts are in the collection of the International Quilt Center & Museum in Lincoln, Nebraska. https://www.tcd.ie/Library/manuscripts/book-of-kells.php.

23. Unpublished artist's statement.

24. Ibid.

25. James, "Mary Catherine Lamb," 14.

26. Robert Shaw, email to the author, November 8, 2014.

27. Ibid.

28. Robert Shaw, "Five Decades of Unconventional Quilts," *Quilter's Newsletter Magazine*, (September 2004), 47.

29. James, phone interview by the author, April 4, 2014.

30. Shaw email to the author.

31. Rauschenberg interview.

32. Articles that feature Mary Catherine Lamb, not otherwise cited in this essay, include:

    Tom Cobb, "Art Choice," *Willamette Week* (April 22–April 28, 1993), 44.

    Elisabeth Dunham, "Mix Master," *Homes and Gardens of the Northwest, The Oregonian* (March 7, 2002), 16–21.

    Bob Hicks, "A Selection of 10 Pieces from The Museum of Contemporary Crafts' '75 Gifts for 75 Years,'" *The Oregonian* (August 19, 2011), A&E 23.

    Susan Knowles, "Myths: New Form, New Function," *Art Papers*, 8, no. 4 (July/August 1994).

    T. Lindberg, "Mary Catherine Lamb: Quiltmaker," *Preview of the Visual Arts* (February/March, 1996).

    Mary Orr, "Mary Catherine Lamb: Fracturing Icons," *Fiberarts* (March/April, 1994), 34.

    Mary Thomas, "Artists Contrast the Secular and the Spiritual," *Pittsburgh Post-Gazette* (July 8, 2000),

    Jason Vondersmith, "Still Living Through Her Quilts," *Portland Tribune* (September 2, 2009).

    Lynn Lewis Young, "Visions: A Review," *Art/Quilt #2* (1995).

33. James phone interview.

34. James, "Mary Catherine Lamb", 14.

35. Nancy Haught, "Quilter Stitches Book of Kells Into Art," *The Oregonian* (November 1, 2001), E1.

36. Unpublished list of exhibitions prepared by the artist, Mary Orr collection.

37. Ibid.

38. Bonnie Laing-Malcolmson, phone interview by the author, February 2, 2016.

39. Nicole Nathan, phone interview by the author, February 2, 2016.

40. Carolyn Ducey, phone interview by the author, February 3, 2016.

41. Ibid.

42. James, phone interview.

43. Joan Harvey, "Life Story: Mary Catherine Lamb. A Woman of Precision," *The Oregonian* (September 13, 2009), B3.

44. Ibid.

45. Ibid.

46. Ibid.

47. Ibid.

48. Ibid.

49. Shaw, email.

50. Constance Van Flandern, "All Together Now," *Budget Living* (December/January 2003), 124–127.

51. Oregon Public Television, "Quilter Mary Catherine Lamb."

52. Ibid.

53. Blair, "Crazy Quilter, Kitsch Queen" and Van Flandern, "All Together Now."

54. Harvey, "Life Story: Mary Catherine Lamb."

55. Mary Orr, interview by the author, April 14, 2014; Rauschenberg interview; Nancy Becker, interview by the author, April 22, 2014.

56. Christopher Rauschenberg and Susan Seubert, *Mary Catherine Lamb's House* (Self-published), 2009.

Contributors

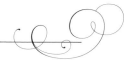

Lynne Zacek Bassett is an award-winning independent scholar specializing in New England's historic costume and textiles. Among her quilt publications and exhibitions are *Northern Comfort: New England's Early Quilts, 1780–1850,* produced for Old Sturbridge Village in 1998, and *Telltale Textiles: Quilts from the Historic Deerfield Collection* (2002). Lynne was the editor and primary author of *Massachusetts Quilts: Our Common Wealth* (2009). In 2012 appeared *Homefront & Battlefield: Quilts & Context in the Civil War,* co-authored by Bassett and Madelyn Shaw and published by the American Textile History Museum. Bassett holds a BA in American studies from Mount Holyoke College and a MA in costume and textile history from the University of Connecticut.

Diana Bell-Kite is an associate curator at the North Carolina Museum of History in Raleigh, and an adjunct lecturer in the graduate program in museum studies at the University of North Carolina at Greensboro. She holds a master of arts in American history from the College of William & Mary. At the museum, Bell-Kite has curated or co-curated multiple exhibitions, including *Everyday Artistry* (2008), which spotlighted Tar Heel quilting, *The Story of North Carolina* (2011), the museum's 20,000-square-foot centerpiece chronological history exhibition, and *Made Especially for You by Willie Kay* (2016), which chronicles the extraordinary career of North Carolina's preeminent formalwear designer of the twentieth century.

Jonathan Gregory earned his MA in textile history with an emphasis on quilt studies from the University of Nebraska-Lincoln in 2007 and his PhD in Human Sciences with a specialization in textiles, also from UNL, in 2015. In 2010, Gregory became Assistant Curator of Exhibitions at the International Quilt Study Center & Museum, in Lincoln, Nebraska, where he leads development and production of exhibitions. Gregory is co-editor of the IQSC&M's website, *World Quilts: The American Story,* and is a contributing author to various IQSC&M publications, including *American Quilts in the Industrial Age, 1790–1870* (2017), *What's in a Name* (2012), *American Quilts in the Modern Age, 1870–1940* (2009), and *Pojagi: Patchwork from Korea* (2008).

Colleen Hall-Patton teaches women's studies at the College of Southern Nevada and sociology at University of Nevada Las Vegas. She graduated with a PhD in sociology from UNLV in 2004. Her dissertation *(Quilters Between Revivals: The Cultural Context of Quilting, 1945–1970)* used quilting to look at changes in women's roles, the relation of gender and art, and the impact of commercialization in the twenty-five years after World War II. This paper is partially derived from that research. Her BA and master's degrees are in anthropology from UCLA, where she researched contemporary quilters. Her areas of interest are in the arts, history, gender, globalization, cultural studies, celebrity studies, and cultural change.

Peggy Hazard is an art exhibition curator and quiltmaker in Tucson, Arizona, whose art history M. A. thesis surveyed local African-American quiltmakers. Over a nineteen-year career at Tohono Chul Park, she curated nearly 100 exhibitions portraying the diverse cultures and artists of the southwestern United States, including exhibitions of historic and contemporary quilts and needlework. She served on the planning committees for the *Patterns of the Past* quilt history conferences (1996, 1998, and 2001) in Tucson and presented *From Cactus Needles to Quilting Needles,* examining botanical-themed quilts in Arizona. Currently, Peggy is an independent curator, a member of the Arizona Quilt Study Group, and an active volunteer with the Tucson Quilt Documentation team.

Sandy Staebell received a BA in history from the University of Northern Iowa in 1980 and a master's in museum science from Texas Tech University three years later. She has been the Registrar/Curator of the Kentucky Museum, Western Kentucky University since 1988. She currently holds the rank of Associate Professor in Library Special Collections. Her research interests include quilts, historic costuming, political memorabilia, and decorative arts.

Susan Stanley holds a BA in English from the University of Nebraska (1964). In 2015, she was awarded a master's degree in the history of textiles with an emphasis on quilt studies from the University of Nebraska-Lincoln. As a teenager, her fascination with quilts was ignited in a Lincoln Goodwill store while excavating a tied quilt made of cotton feed sack. Picking out the yarn ties revealed its secret batting: an intact late nineteenth-century Ohio Star quilt with long-faded indigo blue prints. Decades later, Susan made her first quilt, an Ohio Star incorporating ninety-eight different calicoes snipped from her own clothing, and from her young daughters' homemade dresses. It took three years to complete. Researching and writing about quilts, she concluded, beats making them.

Index

In Appreciation

The American Quilt Study Group expresses sincere appreciation to the following for their substantial support of Seminar presentations and underwriting of papers presented in this volume.

Arizona Quilters Hall of Fame

Pete & Linda Claussen

Marianne Fons in honor and recognition of quilter Vonda Davis

Friends of Mary Catherine Lamb

The Robert & Ardis James Foundation

Lone Star Quilt Study Group

Midwest Fabric Study group in honor of Jean Odom

The Presidential Medallion Quilt Study Project and the Connecticut Quilt
    Study Days

Professional Association of Appraisers—Quilted Textiles (PAAQT)

Elizabeth Jill Wilson

Color Plates

Color plate 1. Peggy Hazard, Suzanne Hesh, & Alice Vinson, *2005–2006 Migrant Quilt*, 2010. Canvas and denim jeans with shirts, bandanas, embroideries, cloth and paint. 86 1/2 x 60 inches. Wilson Graham Photography.

Color plate 2. Cornelia Bayley, *2010–2011 Migrant Quilt*, 2014. Denim jeans and cloth with embroideries, beads, milagros, crosses and mixed media. 61 x 54 1/2 inches. Wilson Graham Photography.

Color plate 3. Cornelia Bayley, *2001–2002 Migrant Quilt,* 2014. Denim jeans and cloth with beads, milagros and mixed media. 89 1/2 x 47 inches. Wilson Graham Photography.

Color plate 4. Maker unknown, Strip Quilt, Sanford, North Carolina, 1958. Satin acetate florist ribbon, pieced. 87 1/4 x 82 inches. Made in memory of Margaret Irene Wicker. Collection of the North Carolina Museum of History, Raleigh, NC, 1993.221.1. Photograph by Eric Blevins and D. Kent Thompson.

Color plate 5. Pearl Harris Evans, Lattice Quilt, Macon, North Carolina, c. 1951–1958. Satin acetate florist ribbon, pieced. 63 x 86 inches. Made in memory of Willie Raymond Riggan, North Carolina Quilt Project, courtesy of the North Carolina Museum of History.

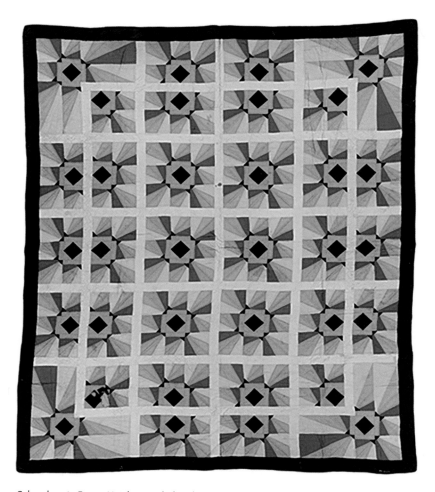

Color plate 6. Ernest Haight, untitled quilt, c. 1935–1940. Private Collection. Image by the author and courtesy of the International Quilt Study Center & Museum.

Color plate 7. Ernest Haight, *Grandmother's Old-Fashioned Nosegay* quilt, c. 1960. Private Collection. Image by the author and courtesy of the International Quilt Study Center & Museum.

Color plate 8. Mildred Potter Lissauer, *Godey Quilt,* 1933–1934. 102 x 91 3/4 inches.
Kentucky Museum, Western Kentucky University (WKU), 1990.6.1.

Color plate 9. Attributed to Mildred Woods Bagby, *Flower Baskets* Quilt, late 1920s–early 1930s. 104 1/2 x 87 3/4 inches. Kentucky Museum, WKU, 1990.6.5.

Color plate 10. Mildred Potter Lissauer, *Godey Quilt,* detail. Adapted from several design sources, this appliqué manifests the success of the collaboration between Lissauer and Rigsby.

Color plate 11. Mildred Potter Lissauer, *Godey Quilt*, detail. Lissauer specified the embellishments Ollie Rigsby added to the "flower box ladies" appliqués in row 5. Kentucky Museum, WKU 1990.6.1.

Color plate 12. Mary Catherine Lamb, *Saint Anthony's Torment*, 1993. 68 x 48 inches.
Collection of Christopher Rauschenberg and Janet Stein. Photograph by Christopher
Rauschenberg.

Color plate 13. Mary Catherine Lamb, *The Archangel Michael Bids You Aloha,* 1991. Silk, brocade, cotton, beads, plastic ribbon, and transit tokens. 55 1/4 x 38 1/2 inches. Portland Art Museum, Portland, Oregon. Gift of Nancy Becker, 2011.81. Photograph by Christopher Rauschenberg.

Color plate 14. Mary Catherine Lamb, *The Four Horsemen of the Apocalypse*, 1995. 80 x 60 inches. International Quilt Study Center & Museum, 2006.043.00042

Color plate 15. Mary Catherine Lamb, *Mark the Lion*, 2000. 53 x 33 inches. International Quilt Study Center & Museum, 2010.009.0003.

Color plate 16. Mary Catherine Lamb, *Sock Monkey Jamboree*, 2007. 64 x 45 inches. International Quilt Study Center & Museum, 2007.043.0001.